JACKIE ROBINSON'S
Little League Baseball Book

JACKIE ROBINSON'S

Little League Baseball Book

by

Jackie Robinson

•

PRENTICE-HALL, INC., Englewood Cliffs, N.J.

ISBN 0-13-509232-9
Library of Congress Catalog Card Number: 74-158193
Printed in the United States of America   T

Prentice-Hall International, Inc., London
Prentice-Hall of Australia, Pty. Ltd., Sydney
Prentice-Hall of Canada, Ltd., Toronto
Prentice-Hall of India Private Ltd., New Delhi
Prentice-Hall of Japan, Inc., Tokyo

Third Printing........May, 1972

Acknowledgment

A word of thanks to Joe Carter whose professional help was invaluable in writing this book.

CONTENTS

●●●●●●●●●●●●●●●●

1

●●●●●●●●●●●●●●●●●●●●●●●●

INTRODUCTORY THOUGHTS

The reason that I'm so firmly convinced of the value of Little League baseball—in fact, the reason that I decided to write this book—is not because I'm a former major league ball player myself, but because I feel that Little League ball, properly coached and played, is of inestimable value in helping to shape the lives of youngsters for their entire future.

I like to tell the Little Leaguers I meet that they're basically in the same position as a major leaguer going to Spring training. The major leaguer knows that whether he has a good year or a bad one depends not only on his natural ability, but also on his physical condition, and Spring training is the time that he has to get himself into the best possible physical shape. It is a period of laying the foundation for the strength he will need in the months to come.

And that is what I think playing Little League ball should do for youngsters—lay the foundation for the years ahead of them, not just in baseball, but for their entire lives. I do not look on the Little League as a juvenile training ground for possible future major leaguers—nor does the Little League itself think that way.

It's own charter says, in part, that its purpose is "To help and voluntarily assist boys in developing qualities of citizenship, sportsmanship, and manhood." Professional baseball —even down at the minor league level—demands such a

1

high level of physical skills and ability that, if a Little Leaguer gets to play pro ball it is due far more to the capabilities of the body he was born with, rather than anything the Little League was able to teach him.

Little League ball is none the less important for that, however.

In this introductory chapter I would like to touch briefly on a number of points that I will go into later in greater detail:

1. ATTITUDE
2. BE YOURSELF
3. WHAT POSITION TO PLAY
4. PHYSICAL CONDITION
5. PRACTICE
6. DESIRE
7. PHILOSOPHY
8. WHAT MANAGERS LOOK FOR
9. WINNING

Attitude

The first basic that determines a boy's ability to play ball —assuming that he has the prime physical abilities—is his attitude. A boy's attitude determines almost everything he does, from the way he plays baseball to the way he lives his life.

It is compounded of many things. Part of it is determined by his life at home, how his parents think and react. Part of it is determined by other facets of his life—the sort of kids he goes around with, even how well he is doing in school. (Parenthetically I would say to youngsters that how well you do in school can affect how well you play ball. When I was going to high school and to college, I found that if I was doing well in my studies, I played better ball. If I was doing poorly, I found myself brooding over my language grade instead of trying to figure out what the next pitch was going to be.)

The reason that I put attitude first is that it applies to all boys alike, regardless of whether nature has given one a good strong body and great natural gifts, or another a body that isn't as strong and who doesn't have those inborn talents.

A great natural player with the wrong attitude isn't going very far, whether it's in baseball or in life.

When you see a Little League player—or any player, for that matter—after he's hit a routine ground ball to the infield, always sort of loafing down to first, you know right then that he'll never become a top player, no matter how talented he is. The sort of player who legs it out only when his teammates yell at him.

On the other hand, a less talented player with a strong and driving attitude is the one who'll win out.

When I'm talking about attitude, I'm really talking about two things at the same time.

One is determination: The drive to play the very best ball you can, all the time, to put out to the best of your ability regardless of what the odds seem.

I remember one of the greatest plays I ever saw Willie Mays make—and, as you know, he's made thousands of them—was in the old Polo Grounds in New York in 1951. It seemed that the odds against making the play were a thousand to one. A ball was hit to right center field so far away from Willie that it seemed impossible that any living man could get to it, yet he tore over there as hard as he could go, leapt for the ball, speared it at the very last split second, planted his right foot, spun his body almost completely around as he was getting the ball out of his glove, and then threw out Billy Cox at home plate.

Red Smith, the famous sports columnist for the New York *Herald Tribune*, wrote the next day that it seemed as if Willie "had raced a mile and a half and then leaped twenty feet through the air" to get the ball.

That was the way Mays was. He absolutely never gave up, no matter what the odds seemed, and that play he made is still referred to as one of the greatest single plays in baseball. His throw was the difference between the Giants winning or losing that game, I think, and it might have been the difference between them winning or losing the pennant, too.

The second factor in attitude is the ability to accept defeat: No matter how much you want to win, or how well you play, a team or a player is going to have defeats. The important thing is how you take them.

My advice is, when you are defeated, sure you'll be disappointed, but after the initial disappointment is over, just resolve that from here on, you're going to try even harder.

I still remember very clearly that 1951 pennant race, when my team, the Brooklyn Dodgers, were tied with the New York Giants in the very last game of the play-off series. Everything depended on the outcome of that last game. We went into the last inning leading by three runs. The Giants scored a run. Then, with two men on base, our pitcher, Ralph Branca, threw a high inside pitch to Bobby Thomson, and Thomson hit the ball into the left field stands for a home run. We lost, five to four, and with the game went the pennant.

After we got over our first shock, we took the attitude well good luck to Thomson, but we're going to do our level best never to be in that situation again, where one pitch can cost us the pennant.

We went down to Spring training the next year with the attitude that we were going to play all-out ball from the very first game, to play every game as hard as we knew how. Then maybe when we came down to the end of the season we would have enough of a lead so that the outcome of the entire season would not depend on what happened in the final game.

We did, too. We won the pennant four times in the next five years, and in 1955 we won the World Series.

I remember another thing about that 1951 game. After it was over, Branca was sitting in his car outside the ball park, crying. A Catholic priest saw him and walked over to try to console him. Finally Branca said:

"Father, why did this have to happen to me?"

The priest said: "My boy, perhaps it was because God knew that you had the strength to handle it."

Perhaps that's why tough things happen to you, too, because you have the strength to handle them.

In addition to the youngsters, I think parents should also have the right attitude toward Little League ball, because parents play the most important role in developing their boy's attitude, in the home, around the dinner table. Too many parents, I believe, are overly concerned about winning, about winning every game.

Too many parents reward a boy for playing a good game, or being on a winning team. They withhold the reward when he plays badly or his team loses. The important thing is for the parents to give the boy encouragement, to let him know they're behind him all the time, good, bad, or indifferent. I remember my wife and I had a terribly difficult time when our older son got involved with narcotics. He was under enormous pressures that were not of his own making; but we stood by him all the way, giving him all the help and assistance we could. In the end it paid off in our relationship with him, and in his own emotional growth and understanding of himself. So, to develop the correct attitude in a youngster, the parents need to have the correct attitude.

Let him know that you're on his side. If he strikes out at a crucial point in a ball game, he undoubtedly feels worse about it than you do. Don't criticize him for it. You can't tell him it didn't mean anything, because he knows better, but you can try to soften it for him. Let him know that it's part of the game, plenty of major leaguers have struck out with the bases loaded, maybe the next time, the luck of the game will be with him.

Be Yourself

I remember when I was a youngster I very much wanted to be a ball player, I'd see an older fellow, in college or in pro ball, and wonder if I'd ever be that good. But then I realized after a while that what you have to do is to play, day after day, in your own way, playing up to your capabilities, and stop worrying that you can't throw as hard, or run as fast, as a boy two or three years older than yourself.

You must, however, play up to the utmost of your capacity. If a boy can run a hundred yards in fifteen seconds, he shouldn't waste time worrying that he can't run it in fourteen, that some boy a little older can. On the other hand, he should never let up so that he finds himself running it in sixteen.

It's something like what you may have noticed when you've been out for a drive in a car. Off in the distance you see a hill so steep that you wonder if the car can really make it. But as you get closer, as you come to the bottom of the hill, you see that the grade seems less and less steep, and the car goes up it with no trouble at all.

It's the same thing in baseball. If you look at a really good ball player who is a few years older than you are, you think to yourself that he's so much better than you, and you'll never get to be that good. But as you get closer and closer to his age, if you just keep on playing, day by day and game by game, you'll find that it isn't nearly as tough as it seemed at first.

I'd like to make another point about being yourself, and this is it: Don't try to model yourself after another player, whether it's the boy a few years older than you or some major leaguer you admire. Don't try to be another Mickey

Mantle or Joe DiMaggio or Willie Mays or Carl Yastrzemski. Play your own way. Swing the bat your own way.

If you have the power to hit home runs, go ahead and swing in the way that gets those home runs. But remember, a lot of batters, even up in the big leagues, are not home-run hitters. Look at Matty Alou. He's a spray hitter, he hits to all fields. He doesn't try to overpower the ball because he's being himself. He knows his own abilities, and he knows that he's a line-drive hitter.

I remember a player named Tommy Brown on the Dodgers. Tommy admired DiMaggio so much that if you saw him from a distance you'd think he was DiMaggio—by the way he walked, from the way he swung the bat, even from the way he wore his cap. Except that he couldn't hit like DiMaggio; and I thought a number of times that I ought to tell him, Tommy, you're thinking about DiMaggio so much that you're forgetting yourself. You're forgetting about the basic thing, that you're supposed to be playing baseball—your own way.

I'm a great admirer of DiMaggio myself, I know he's one of the greatest ball players of all time, but it never crossed my mind for a moment to think of trying to imitate him. As maybe I should have told Brown, when you're playing ball, play it your own way.

What Position to Play

Part of being yourself is deciding where you want to play in baseball. Some boys are born with naturally quick hands and quick reflexes, they're able to get quick starts on batted balls, and boys like that, I believe, should first of all think of the infield. Some boys are rangy and can cover a lot of ground; they should think of the outfield. Some boys just naturally like to catch, they like the action that goes on around home plate.

I haven't mentioned pitching because I regard that as the manager's prerogative; in Little League the manager obviously wants the strongest boys, the hardest throwers— who can get the ball over the plate—on his pitching staff.

One of the first things you should do is to find out what you *can* do and what each position on the team demands. Then decide on what your abilities are, what position you're best suited to play, and devote yourself to it.

This doesn't mean that at ten, eleven or twelve you're making a life-time decision; at fourteen or fifteen you may find that you like another position better, or you can play another position better, and you should switch over.

But if you learn early enough what position you want to play and can play best—even in general terms like between playing in the infield or the outfield—and you work consistently at improving yourself at that position, you'll end up that much better a player.

Sometimes physical circumstances determine your choice. If you want to be an infielder and you're left handed, for example, you know right off the bat that the only place you can play is first base and that catching is out.

Generally speaking, you'll find that you're best at the first position you started at. It's probably because you liked that position best, and therefore you probably practiced it more.

A player who can move around a lot, from position to position, can have a very special value to a team. It's especially true in Little League, where you may be playing at shortstop one inning and in center field the next. It's also true in the majors, though in the majors it generally means that you're going to be used as a substitute as much as you can.

As soon as you can, try to concentrate on really learning one or two positions. After all, learning to be a top-notch second baseman is a full-time career. As I said, the player who can move around can be a very valuable asset to a team, but on the other hand, he never really gets to be out-standing at any one position.

If you are going to shift around, even in Little League, I'd suggest that you try to get one or two positions down solid. Each position has its own demands, each position requires you to do things in a different way. To give just one example: the throw that an infielder has to make on a ground ball is entirely different from the throw an outfielder makes. An infielder has to be able to make a lot of quick starts and stops, but an outfielder rarely has to.

All this, as I said, is just part of getting to know yourself on the baseball field.

Physical Condition

When you're in Little League, you should just naturally be in fine physical condition. Just being ten, eleven or twelve years old means you run a lot, you get a lot of exercise one way or another. Your mother probably sees that you have the right food to eat and that you get enough sleep. In fact, about the only things I can think of that you can do wrong is staying up too late watching television, or filling yourself up all the time on hot dogs and popcorn and soda pop.

I hope you'll remember this as you get older. I remember my career in athletics was shaped, in part, by some advice my high school coach, Newt Stark, gave me very early in my playing days. That advice influenced my attitude toward taking care of myself more than anything else I can think of.

Stark told me that unless I was willing to stay away from smoking and drinking, my chances of being a good athlete would be infinitely reduced. I know that smoking and drinking is hardly a problem among Little Leaguers, but I'd like to emphasize it's not too early to recognize that, to be any kind of athlete, you have to learn to take care of your own body. And to stick with it as you grow up.

Practice

I'll get to team practice later, but in this chapter I'd like to mention the practice a Little Leaguer can get in on his own, or with his friends or members of his family—his brother or brothers, if he has any, or his father.

In practice I'd like to include reading, which tells you what you can do, or what other players have done, and so contributes to your understanding of the game. A Little Leaguer should read everything he can about the game. By all odds, he should read two booklets published by Little League Baseball, Inc., at Williamsport, Pennsylvania, one of which gives the rules and regulations of Little League ball, the other gives an excellent basic description of the theory of how to play ball.

Theory is not enough, however, and that is where practice comes into play.

Even a youngster who doesn't have great natural baseball skills can develop himself into a good ball player if he has the other qualities I've mentioned—a basically sound body, the right attitude, the desire, the ambition to learn all that he can about baseball, the will to practice as much as he can.

I think a perfect example of my point is Eddie Stanky. Eddie wasn't one of the great natural ball players. He wasn't graceful and easy. He couldn't cover ground the way other major league infielders could, whether he was in the field or on base. He couldn't make double plays with the ease of other major league infielders.

And with all that against him, he ended up being an established major league player whose name is familiar to everyone interested in baseball.

Stanky was determined to be a major league ball player

from the time he was a youngster. He tried to learn everything he could about the game. Then he went out and practiced and practiced till he couldn't practice any more.

He also used his brains, and using your brains can make up for a lot of deficiencies in baseball. I remember Branch Rickey once said of Stanky: "Every time he gets out on the field, he figures out a new way to beat you."

There are a lot of top ball players who have such great natural talents that they never learn baseball technically, say, the way an engineer learns to build bridges. You think of the legendary names, the Babe Ruths and the Ted Williamses, they all had the natural physical equipment to be great ball players: the coordination and the reflexes, the muscle and the strength. Their ability to hit the long ball, or to hit consistently over .300, insured their careers. If you turn out to be a player like that, you're one of the lucky few.

But if you're an average youngster starting out in the Little League at the age of ten—and this goes even if you are better than average physically—if you want to become one of the top players on your team or in your league in the next couple of years, you ought to take a leaf out of Stanky's book. Because, as I say, he *learned* baseball.

Part of learning baseball is to start figuring out everything that can possibly happen on the field, and what you should do in any given situation. If you start doing that early, you'll soon find that things just seem to happen naturally, and you can be more relaxed.

A relaxed player is a much better player. How many times have you seen a Little League infielder standing there holding the ball while an opposing player slides into second or third—a player who would have been an easy out if the infielder had simply thrown to the base? It's simply because the infielder hadn't figured out beforehand what he was supposed to do if such-and-such a thing happened.

When he saw the play developing, he simply froze.

Good players figure out before every pitch what they're going to do if the ball is hit to them—and what they're going to do if it's hit somewhere else. After all, on every pitch there are only a few options. The batter is either going to hit it or he isn't, and if he hits it, it's either going to you or somewhere else. Being prepared for what may happen eliminates doubt in your mind and makes the play that much easier.

To help you out, you should start learning your team's signals as soon as you can. I know that there are only a few signals in Little League, but it's good practice to know them. Even if they are only signals for a bunt or a steal, if you know them it helps to keep you aware of what's going on in the game.

And if your team is good enough so that the pitcher and catcher use signals—again, if it's only the difference between a fast ball and a change-up—the play that develops will not come as a surprise to you.

This is especially true for infielders, and it will grow increasingly important as you move up in baseball. It is an enormous advantage for a major league infielder, for example, to know whether the pitch coming up is going to be a fast ball or a curve. It gives him an edge over the hitter in knowing where to play the ball, and many times it will make the difference between the ball that's caught and the ball that goes through to the outfield for a base hit.

I myself think it's a good idea for a team to have a few basic signs, even down at the Little League level, because it can be helpful in keeping the players alert, and in training them for what they're going to face if they go on to the Babe Ruth League or into high school ball.

It's very unlikely that the outcome of a Little League game will hinge on whether a shortstop knew that the pitcher was going to throw one kind of pitch as opposed to another, but even in Little League you should at least be aware of some of these kinds of sophistication in playing baseball.

I also think that having a few signals in Little League adds a little professional touch to the game that all Little Leaguers really like.

What you *must* do in Little League, once the pitcher starts his throwing motion, is to figure that the ball is going to be hit to you. You have to be on your toes. Even if it isn't hit to you, you've got to figure you'll be in every play that develops, and you've got to plan ahead what you're going to do if the ball is hit here or hit there.

If you're playing third or short, figure that the ball is going to be belted straight at you as hard as the batter can hit it. I'll go more into that later, but I think that a ball hit straight to you, hard, is one of the toughest of all plays for an infielder to make. You've just got to be ready for it all the time.

If you really want to become a good player, you've got to imagine all these things happening to you in advance, and figure out what you're going to do if this or that happens. On the ball field, and in a game, is no place for a player to start wondering what he's going to do.

You don't need a whole ball field and a squad of players if you want to practice. If you want to practice fielding on your own, all you need is a backyard or a school playground, and someone to hit fungoes. If you want to practice throwing, all you need is a target and a backstop.

Once, an old-time big league player with a deadly throwing arm said that he learned to throw when he was a boy on the farm. When he was supposed to be hoeing corn or something, he'd set up a pail on top of a fence and get some stones and turn his back on the pail. Then he'd suddenly whirl and throw as fast and as hard as he could till he got so that he could hit the pail pretty frequently from a hundred feet away. (If you're going to try this, I recommend plenty of clear space around the target. Don't set it up twenty feet from somebody's living room window.) I cite this just to make it clear that if you have the ambition to learn to throw, you don't need a lot of fancy equipment.

If you want to practice pitching, get yourself some string and two poles. (You can use two trees if they fit the bill, or a couple of gateposts.) Tie two strings horizontally, one at the level of your knees and one at the level where the letters on your uniform would be. Then tie two more strings vertically (up and down) between the first two, and the width of home plate—seventeen inches. You now have a strike zone, and all you need is a backstop and some baseballs. Mark off a line forty-six feet away from your strike zone (the regulation distance), and throw from behind that.

As you can see, there's no trick at all to figuring out a way to practice.

Desire

You won't practice much if you don't have desire, because desire is what motivates everything you do—in baseball as well as in life.

If a young fellow doesn't really burn to play ball, if he isn't just crazy to get out there and play—and even practice —he isn't going to make it. There are hundreds of thousands of youngsters in this country, not to mention countries like Mexico and Japan, where our style of ball is taking hold, who do have the real desire to play.

Every youngster starting out in baseball is automatically in competition with others, and the amount of desire is frequently the determining factor between who plays and who doesn't. It comes from a feeling deep within yourself. If you don't feel this way about playing ball, you might as well forget it. Such a youngster might be able to get by for a while as a so-so player if he has the basic skills, but without the desire he'll never be any better than a small-time player.

Desire can come with playing, of course. Some youngsters start out in Little League just because their friends are
trying out, or because the other fellows are on the team and
they have no one to play with. But they find, the more they
play the better they like it, and pretty soon they're as much
charged up as anyone else.

Desire is very much tied in with practice. What drove
Eddie Stanky was desire. And I remember reading that Pa-
derewski, the great pianist, even after he was acknowledged
as one of the outstanding players in the world, used to practice six and seven hours a day. Why? Because, he said, once
you've achieved your skills, you have to keep using them all
the time, otherwise they begin to deteriorate.

Jack Nicklaus the great golfer, said that when he was a
young player just starting out, he would play two practice
rounds a day—thirty-six holes—and then go off to a driving
range and drive two or three hundred balls.

Obviously, in Little League you're not going to practice
on that scale, and you shouldn't. I'd get a little worried myself about a boy who did absolutely nothing except practice
baseball. But you should have enough desire to practice
enough so that you can play up to your best.

Philosophy

By philosophy in baseball, I mean putting things in their
correct perspective.

You should be able to see what you're getting out of the
Little League, even if you aren't one of the guys who's always making the key play, always getting the big hit, always
getting the applause.

For one thing, you should be getting fun out of it. If you
don't really *like* playing ball, I don't think you should do it
for some other reason. And you're learning to get along
with the other players. You're getting into competition for
the first time, and you should like that, too. Most boys I

come in contact with like competition. Little League ball also helps you to handle crises—not major crises, it's true, but crises on the baseball field. You will then develop the ability to handle bigger pressures later on, instead of letting the pressures handle you.

Your baseball philosophy should include the ability to lose. This may sound wrong when you're always being told about the importance of winning. It's certainly not the function of a Little League team to take a group of youngsters and start teaching them how to lose. Sooner or later you have to face the fact that a certain amount of losing is part of life; you're not going to win every game you play. You have to be able to accept it with the thought that you're going to come back the next time and win. In boxing, you know, they say that the real hallmark of a champion is the ability to get up off the floor and come back to win.

I remember that the Little League manager in Stamford, Connecticut, when my oldest son was playing there, had a lot of this philosophy. The manager had never been a professional player—in fact, high school ball was as far as he'd ever gotten—but he had a deep belief that he ought to be doing his part to help youngsters get ready for life.

He didn't have a lot of technical knowledge. He couldn't really tell a youngster the fine points about how to hit a ball or how to field it, because he hadn't actually gone through all that himself—and the only way you really get to know how to play baseball is like anything else, you start as young as you can and do it as much as you can—but he did have the right ideas about winning and losing. "Go all out to win if you can," he'd tell the youngsters playing for him. And if they didn't win, he'd tell them, "never mind, you tried, we'll win the next time."

This manager had a number of other traits that I think should be models for Little League managers everywhere. He didn't act as if he was a high-powered major league manager going into a stretch run for the pennant, snarling the way I've seen some Little League managers do at a boy for missing a play, that maybe a player with ten times his experience couldn't have made.

And he wasn't always trying to impress the kids with how much he knew about baseball. He wasn't afraid to discuss things with his players about what they should do, or what they should have done. When I showed up at a game he'd come over to me, before the game or after, sometimes when the teams were changing sides, and ask me what I thought of such-and-such a play, or what I would have done in such-and-such a situation.

It strikes me that this manager's whole attitude may have subconsciously taught the youngsters a great deal about the proper attitude toward life.

One game that I'll never forget in the Stamford Little League, offers a perfect illustration of a point that should be included in your philosophy of baseball.

The game was very important in the standing of our division, and somewhere along the line the young third baseman made an error that let a run score. After the inning was over he went back to the bench and really broke down. He was sitting on the end of the bench all by himself, as far away from his teammates as he could get, crying. Finally I went over to talk to him, to give him a chance to pull himself together.

I gave him a little talk that I've frequently given to young players about why they have an "E" column on a scoreboard and in the box scores in the newspapers. It's because they figure no one is perfect, everyone's bound to make an error sooner or later. The important thing for a player to figure out is whether he made, absolutely, the best possible play he could under the circumstances.

If he'd done that, no one could ask anything more of him, but if he'd made a mistake, then what he should do was to try to figure out what the mistake was so that he wouldn't make it again.

The young third baseman and I began to talk about what had happened on that particular play.

How had the ball gotten through him?

What we finally decided, talking together, was that he had allowed the ball to play him, rather than his playing the ball.

I told him that every Little Leaguer, in fact every ball player including the ones in the major leagues, has to learn to accept the fact that, sooner or later, he's going to make an error.

In the Little League, when you're just learning how to play the game, maybe you haven't yet been taught all the fine little details on how to play, where to throw under every possible combination of circumstances, so you're naturally going to make more mistakes than a more experienced player. Nobody wants to make an error, of course, and every player always feels bad after an error, but you can't afford to let it get you down too much.

If you really let yourself get down after you've made a bad throw or committed some other error, that's when you're most likely to make more errors because you've gotten yourself into an error-making frame of mind. The thing to do is to forget the error and concentrate on the next play.

The attitude to take is, okay, I made an error, but I've seen Brooks Robinson make an error and he's probably the best fielding third baseman in the major leagues. What I've got to do is to get set so that I don't make another one on the next play.

Which is what you're likely to do if you're still thinking about the first one.

And afterwards, don't alibi. It's no use. Everyone on the field knows whether you made an error or not. If you made it, you made it, and that's that. Don't try to explain it away by saying that the ball took a bad hop.

To get back to my young third baseman at Stamford, I explained all that to him, but I also emphasized that, as a fielder, he hadn't started to move soon enough and fast enough when the ball had been hit.

That advice goes whether you're an infielder or an outfielder, although an outfielder has a better chance of correcting himself if he starts off wrong, simply because it takes the ball that much longer to get to him. An infielder really has to start moving at almost the instant the ball leaves the bat. He has to charge the ball so that he can play it on the hop he wants to get it on, instead of waiting for the ball to get out to him.

What Managers Look For

A good manager can tell in about ten minutes of watching a young prospect whether he has the makings of a good player.

There are three things a manager looks for in a ball player:

The first is *speed,* and the ability to use that speed. In the Little League, the manager isn't expecting to find players who can run the hundred in twelve seconds, all he wants is a player who will run as hard as he can all the time he's playing, one who never stops trying.

The second ability is *throwing.* The manager wants players with the strongest arms he can find. As I've already mentioned, you can develop your throwing by practicing all by yourself, and with practice comes both strength and accuracy.

The third is *power.* A youngster who has power is a much sought-after player. Your power gets greater, of course, as you grow up, but a lot of power comes from smoothness, and this comes from coordination. You can develop this yourself, too, if you have someone who will pitch to you. I'll go into this in greater detail in my section on hitting, but I'd just like to mention there is a "hitting area" in baseball, which extends to about a foot in front of where the bat actually makes contact with the ball. You should time your swing so that you have every ounce of power behind your bat when it gets into that hitting area. It's all a matter of the smoothness, the coordination that you learn through practice.

In hitting, it's not how big and strong you are, it's whether you have complete control of your swing when the bat comes into contact with the ball. Stan Musial was an example of that. He wasn't a tremendously big or strong man, but when his bat came around he was so concentrated and so well-coordinated that he seemed to explode with power. I've seen him hit the ball distances that you just wouldn't believe, looking at his size.

Winning

I believe that baseball, like practically everything else in life, is a game of winning. It's true that it may just be a game, but in that respect it's related to all of life. For the individual player, it means wanting to be the best player on his team—to be the best player on the field. The individual has to want to be a top performer, to give his very best to every play. He's got to come out onto the field determined to win.

This naturally means that the individual player has to be competitive. If you're the pitcher, you have to think, as the batter steps into the box, *this* guy I can get out. Even if he got a hit the last time, you think, *this* time, he's out. You know the batter is determined in the exact opposite way, he's determined that he's going to get a hit.

If you're a fielder, you should be thinking, let him hit it to me, *make* him hit it to me, I can get him out. That's how a winner thinks, that's how you make yourself into a winner.

When you get all your skills under control: your speed, your reflexes, your hitting, your throwing, and then you start thinking like that, that's when you're on your way to becoming a winning player. That's how you play winning Little League ball.

Even if things are going against you, figure that you can come back and win. Of course it doesn't always happen, but if you're thinking that way, if you believe in yourself, you'll find it happens more often than you would have guessed. Strangely enough, thinking that way seems to make the breaks go with you. Start thinking, well, we've lost this one, and you'll find the breaks going against you.

One of the things that made my oldest boy a pretty fair ball player in his younger days with the Little League was this tremendous confidence in himself. Sometimes I used to marvel. I remember twice, in the mornings before play-off games, he'd tell his mother and me, "You know, I'm going to get some hits today"—and two years running he did just that. One year he hit a home run, and the next year he got a single, and both of those hits won games. You can't over-estimate confidence—not bragging, confidence.

That is the note on which I'd like to end this chapter.

If you've got the confidence that you *can* do it, you *will* do it. You can amaze yourself at what you can do. Don't ever say to yourself, I'm not good enough. There will be balls hit that you think you'll never in this world catch— and you'll catch them. But not if you don't think you've got a prayer. There are going to be games where, along toward the final innings, it will look as if you can't possibly win them—and you'll find that you can.

If you don't learn anything else from Little League ball, you'll have learned it all if you learn that confidence can make you a winner.

Never give up.

2
●●●●●
HITTING

To me, hitting is the most interesting and exciting part of baseball.

There are three major factors involved in hitting:

1. YOUR EYES
2. YOUR STANCE
3. YOUR SWING

There are also some general points to be made, which I'll get to at the end of the chapter.

Your Eyes

I can't stress too much the importance of that phrase you've undoubtedly heard ten thousand times: Keep your eye on the ball.

I'd like to explain in detail what I mean. I don't mean you "sort of" follow the flight of the ball. I mean that you concentrate on it. When you're in the batter's box you should have your eyes burned on that ball from the moment it leaves the pitcher's hand. You should be able to see the seams spinning.

And keep your eye on the ball *all* the way in—not part way.

Just watch the hitters in any big league ball game,

whether you're out in the park or watching the game on television.

Not only does the big league hitter focus on the ball from the instant it leaves the pitcher's hand, but he watches it so intently that even after he's hit it, he's still looking down at the spot where the bat made contact.

I remember watching the 1969 play-off games between the Atlanta Braves and the New York Mets on television. In one of the games, Hank Aaron hit a home run for the Braves. Immediately afterwards, the television people ran a slow-motion replay.

It was really an eye-opener. It showed Aaron getting set, it showed his ferociously powerful swing, it showed the bat hitting the ball, but most important of all it showed how Aaron's head was still looking down, his eye right on the spot where the bat hit the ball, even when he was almost halfway through his swing.

His head didn't turn until the momentum of his arms on the follow-through actually physically pulled his head up. You're not going to have a swing like Hank Aaron's in the Little League, but the principle of the way you use your eyes is the same.

And the same thing is true in all sports, not just baseball. For example, if any of you have ever watched professional golf on television you've seen the golfer, when he's putting, spend a lot of time figuring out the green, the roll, the distance and all the rest, then finally set himself to make the putt. And, if you watch closely, you see that just for a second after he's made the putt, his eyes are still focussed on the point where the putter head made contact with the ball.

Every boy I know has watched big-time football, either on the field or television, and how many times have you seen a receiver who looks as though he can't possibly miss catching a pass, bobble it when he actually had it in his hands? It's because at that very last fraction of a second, when he was sure he had the ball, he turned his eyes to see whether there was a tackler coming up, or where he was going to run.

The point of all this is that no matter what kind of ball game you're playing—baseball or football or golf—where play depends on focussing on the ball, if you turn your head even a fraction of a second before you've made actual contact with the ball, or at the very instant that you are making contact, the chances are that you'll take your eye off the ball.

At the very least it means you won't make contact correctly and more often than not, in baseball, it means you miss the ball entirely and end up with a strike.

It's an easy mistake to make, too, especially if it's a tight situation—say, with a man on third and two out. The thing to do is to learn to concentrate when you're at bat. When the pitcher is ready to throw to you, forget everything else going on on the field.

Your Stance

The most important thing about your stance is that it should fit you. If you think about it for a minute, you'll realize that every good hitter in the major leagues has a stance slightly different than the next fellow's—some a lot different. The reason is very simple. No two men are built exactly the same way. Just as no two men have exactly the same fingerprints, no two bodies are the same.

For years, players talked about Willie Davis of the Los Angeles Dodgers. Many of the other players felt that with his great talent, his speed, and what appeared to be a good swing at the ball, he should be a really great hitter.

In my opinion, in the years when he was beginning, Willie's great problem was his stance—or rather the fact that he had too many stances. Sometimes it seemed as if he was in a different stance every time he came up to the plate; and that's bound to hurt your hitting. The main thing is that

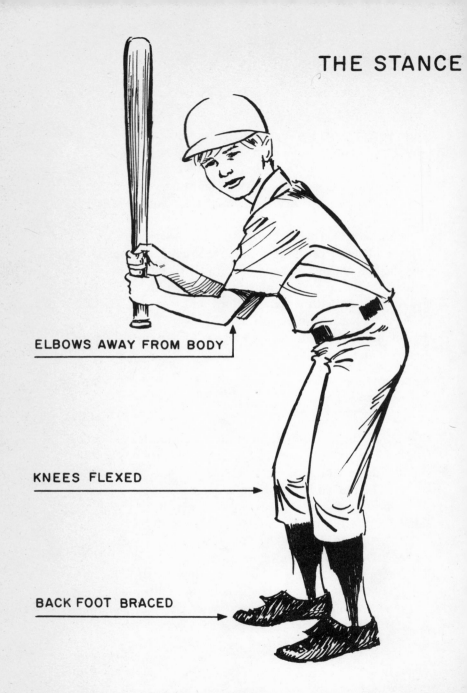

ELBOWS AWAY FROM BODY

KNEES FLEXED

BACK FOOT BRACED

THE STANCE/ Keep elbows away from your body, knees flexed a little and back
foot dug into the dirt. For more control, choke up on the bat.

it spoils your concentration. You're thinking about your stance at the same time you're supposed to be concentrating on the pitch.

In 1969, Davis finally started doing the things that his great talents warranted. He finally chose the stance that was the most comfortable for him, and he stuck to it. This also helped him in other ways. He became a better all-round ball player because his confidence had come back. He knew that with his stance, even if he got into a slump, he would come out of it, so he became a much surer player all the way around.

That's what you should do as a Little Leaguer. Find the stance where you're most comfortable, and stick with it. Step into the batter's box easy and relaxed. Have your elbows away from your body. Have your knees flexed a little. Set yourself so that when you swing, you bring your full weight into the swing. In other words, your weight should be coming forward as you swing, onto the balls of your feet. If you're falling away from the ball, you'll just pop up.

It doesn't matter exactly how you hold your arms, provided they're away from your body. As I said, find your most natural stance. You see Reggie Smith and Carl Yastrzemski of the Boston Red Sox hold their bats very high and I used to hold mine very high when I was playing, but most players don't. But that was the way I felt the most comfortable. It worked for me, it's working for Smith and Yaz, but that doesn't mean that it will work for you.

In setting your stance, the first thing you have to think about is your back foot—your right foot if you're a right-handed hitter, and vice versa. When you're in the batter's box and the pitcher is getting ready to throw to you, you must have your back foot dug into the dirt, and you've got to keep it locked there.

You've seen how a professional football quarterback, when he drops back to pass, has to get his back foot firmly locked against the grass before he throws. That's so he's braced to get his whole body behind his throw, not just his arm, and you have to do the same thing—get your back foot braced so that you can get the full strength of your body behind your swing. If you don't get your back foot planted—or if you come off it—you won't be able to get any power into your swing, you'll be hitting with just your arms.

If, while you're swinging, you come off your front foot, it automatically means that you're hitting off your right foot, which also automatically means that you can't get any distance on the ball at all.

You can prove this point just by watching any major leaguer when he's batting. Don't look at anything except his feet. When the ball is coming in to him, he may move his front foot to step into the ball to get more power. But watch his back foot. It stays dug into the dirt until the force of his swing, as he completes it, pulls the foot away. That's why major league hitters spend so much time digging in around home plate when they come up to bat. They have learned from experience the need of feeling comfortable, of being balanced, of knowing they can't get their full power without being set.

That's also the reason pitchers use the brush-back pitch. They don't want the hitter digging in to the point where he doesn't have to be worried about being brushed back. They want to get the hitter thinking that he can't afford to dig in.

But, you know, it's a duel between the hitter and the pitcher. You, as the hitter, have to watch out for the brush-back pitch, but you can't let the pitcher over-awe you. That's what he wants to do. After a brush-back, you have to get up there and dig yourself in so that you're set to hit. That way, you're playing your game. If you let the pitcher scare you so that you're not digging in, you're playing his game.

I know that when you first come up in the Little League

all the opposing pitchers look as big as Don Newcombe and the ball seems to come in like a rifle shot, but as you play more and more, you'll find that you'll be able to set your stance better and better.

By getting set like that, too, you'll be able to see the ball better. Every time I'm asked about hitting I emphasize how much you have to train your eye, as I did at the beginning of this chapter, but when the pitcher is throwing to you, there's an additional element involved and that's the element of distraction. Don't let his leg kick take your eyes away from picking up his pitching hand as soon as it comes over; once your eyes move, it takes a second to refocus them.

There's another advantage to this: With experience, you'll be able to pick up the rotation of the ball, which way it's spinning, and how fast it's spinning. With experience, you'll be able to figure whether it's a curve or a fast ball, and that's a great advantage to a batter. A good batter can adjust himself to the curve or the fast ball if he picks it up quickly enough.

Of course, refinements like this come only after you've been playing for a while, but it's never too soon to start thinking about it, and watching for it.

Your Swing

The first thing you ought to concentrate on in order to develop a good, smooth swing, is the hitting area (that relatively small bit of space in which the bat meets the ball, maybe a foot from the point where the contact is actually made).

That's where all the elements of your swing have to come together, where your bat has to be traveling at top speed, where you have to have every ounce of your strength behind it. Your swing has to be coordinated so that every bit of your power, from that planted back foot through your

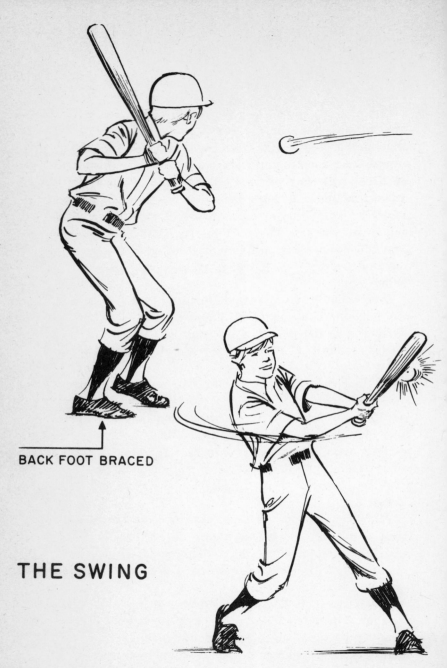

BACK FOOT BRACED

THE SWING

THE SWING /As you swing, your weight should be moving forward onto the balls of your feet, keeping the back foot braced. Time your swing so that full power (from back foot to wrists) is being utilized at the moment of contact. Follow through with your wrists.

whole body down to and including your wrists, is behind the bat when you make contact.

You can't do that at the very instant you start to swing. You have to learn to time yourself, to time your swing so that the bat is going its fastest as it hits the ball. If you're overanxious and try to put everything you have into the top of the swing, you're going to get yourself off-balance, and when you make contact with the ball, providing you *do* make contact with it, you'll probably just pop it up. By trying to hit like that, you actually lose power as you make contact, so that even if you do manage to hit the ball squarely, under those circumstances, the ball won't travel very far.

There's another danger in swinging like that: You're very apt to pull your head, and therefore your eye, off the ball. It's hard enough hitting the ball when you can see it all the way in; it's almost impossible when you pull your head off it.

Again, it's something like golf. You know how frequently you hear an announcer on television say that a golfer has a great, natural, smooth swing, and that's how he gets distance on his drives? Well, you can bet that that golfer didn't get his "great, natural, smooth swing" by just picking up a driver and going out onto the tee and smashing the ball as hard as he could. It took him months and even years of practice.

The principle is the same in baseball. You don't pick up a bat and go out there and try to murder the ball. You go out and swing, and swing as naturally and smoothly as you can until you've gotten it down, until it comes so naturally that you're not even thinking about your swing when you step into the batter's box. If you're just starting out in Little League, I think you should choke up on the bat enough so that you feel you have complete control of it. If you haven't played a lot of ball and you try swinging with the end of the bat, you'll find the bat is playing you, or controlling you, instead of you controlling it.

I mentioned the role of your wrists, and I'd like to go into it a little more. Sometimes, when talking about a major league hitter, other players will say that he gets hits because he has "quick hands." Well, it's the same thing, but I like to think of it as wrist action.

A very important part of a really good swing is the follow-through with the wrists. If you watch a great hitter like Hank Aaron carefully, you'll see that right at the end of his swing, he gets an extra spurt of power by snapping his wrists. That's what you should try to do, too, and you can develop the necessary strength in your wrists by exercising them.

Don't let it worry you if you don't start getting hits right from the very start. Just as at the beginning of Spring training in the major leagues and in the Little League—especially when you're just starting out—the pitchers are always likely to be ahead of you. That's because it always takes hitters a longer time to develop the rhythm of their swing. So don't worry about it. In addition, in the Little League, the pitchers always tend to be the biggest and strongest youngsters on the team.

Even if you go six, seven or eight games without a hit, keep on plugging away. Remember Willie Mays. One of the greatest hitters of all time, but when he first came up to the Giants he went so many at-bats without a hit that he wanted to quit the whole game of baseball. His manager, Leo Durocher, wouldn't let him. He knew Willie had the potential. And if you have a reasonably strong body and reasonably good reflexes, you have the potential to hit Little League pitching.

If you feel discouraged, the first thing you ought to do is talk to your coach. Talk the problem out with him. If he tells you something that disagrees with something you've read, or something you feel, ask him about it. Get it clear in your own mind so that you don't have a lot of conflicting ideas that will only confuse you.

Listening to what your coach has to say can put you miles ahead in the game, because he can see things that others can't. He can see if you're standing with your feet too far apart or not enough. He can see if you're coming off your back foot instead of keeping it firmly planted. He can see if perhaps you're standing too far back in the batter's box so that you can't reach strikes that are thrown away from you.

The pitcher or catcher on your own team—even your own infielders—can't help you as much as your manager or coach because they're not in as good a position to be able to see what you're doing. They're concentrating on the ball, not on you—or they should be. The first thing to do if you feel that you're having trouble is to get your manager to watch you hit in practice, and listen to what he has to say.

If you're just starting out and you're having trouble, he may recommend the use of a batting tee, which is sold in most Sporting Goods stores that carry Little League equipment. This consists of a base made like a home plate, with a flexible hard rubber pole coming up out of the middle of it. The pole is adjustable so that you can move it up and down, and in the top is a kind of shallow cup in which you set the ball. (A baseball is okay if you have a backstop or plenty of room; otherwise I suggest a tennis ball.) The pole is made of hard rubber so that if you hit it instead of the ball, it bends instead of breaking.

I think this is an excellent device to use for practice by yourself if, as I said, you're just starting out and you're having trouble. It obviously isn't as good as having someone pitch to you, but with it you can practice the fundamentals of your swing—getting your back foot set, swinging in a smooth, easy motion.

From there, you can work up to having someone throw to you.

Other Points

A very important part of hitting, if you're to be a fully rounded player and of the greatest value to your club, is the ability to sacrifice.

Take the matter of bunting. There comes a time in almost every game when the manager has to have a bunt. The most familiar situation is in the late innings of a tie game with a man on first and nobody out. That man simply has to get into scoring position on second, and if it's your turn to bat, you should be able to lay down a bunt and not have the manager bring in a pinch hitter for you.

But I've seen even major leaguers foul up a simple play like that. The bunt sign is on and they try to lay one down a couple of times but it doesn't work—the batter fouls them off, or something—so then the bunt sign has to be taken off. Among other things, that forces the manager to change his whole play strategy. And, in those circumstances, the batter then will become so anxious to get a hit that he'll either top the ball for a force at second, or he'll pop-up.

I would say those batters, whether they're in the majors or in the Little League, simply haven't done their job. They didn't work at practicing bunting—and that is something you have to give a little time to. Certainly, a bunt isn't going to raise your batting average, but if you're a team player you have to be willing to do it; and to do it successfully, you have to take the time to learn how to do it.

Actually, the bunt should be the simplest maneuver of all in baseball, because all you have to do is to let the ball hit the bat. There's nothing else to it. You just square around, level your bat, and let the ball hit it.

With a little experience, you'll find that you can steer the ball in the direction you want it to go, either to the right or the left, simply by changing the angle at which you hold the bat as the ball comes in. In other words, in bunting as opposed to hitting away, you can aim the ball.

There's one thing I'd like to emphasize about bunting. Don't try to reach out with your bat to meet the ball. Wait! Let the ball come in to you, holding your bat where you want to. Holding back will give you much better control. Now what could be simpler than just standing there, holding your bat level and aimed the way you want the ball to go?

There's another type of sacrifice that's more complicated and you'll need a little experience to be able to do it successfully, and that's hitting to right.

You probably won't be able to do it with any degree of success until you've gotten to be a more seasoned hitter than you are in Little League, but there's no harm in your knowing about it, if for only one reason: that you know it when a good major league hitter make this type of sacrifice on television. As a matter of fact, there's no harm, in your last year in Little League, if you're a good hitter, in asking your manager how to do it, and trying it a couple of times.

This kind of sacrifice generally comes late in a tie game with nobody out, but now the base runner has to be on second instead of on first. You come up to bat, and your job is to get that man over to third. Now, you know that if you hit to left, the man on second—if he knows his baseball—is not going to be able to start for third until he sees where the ball goes, because he won't know whether the third baseman or the shortstop will be able to field it. So he has to delay starting; and even if the ball does get through to the left fielder, he will move only to third base.

On the other hand, if you can hit to right—unless it's a fly ball, obviously—the runner can start for third almost at the very instant that the ball is hit.

Even if the second baseman can field the ball and you are thrown out at first, you've done your job. This is a real sacrifice. On a sacrifice bunt, you're not charged with a time at bat. On this kind of sacrifice, you are charged with a time at bat, and if you're thrown out, your batting average goes down that much. But even if it does, your manager and your teammates and everyone on the field knows that you've done your job.

Strangely enough, the first piece of advice I got on the importance of this kind of sacrifice was in the Dodgers' locker room in 1947 when we were playing in Boston, and it came from Dixie Walker.

There had been a lot of talk about the fact that Dixie Walker wouldn't even play on the same team with me, since I was the first black player to be signed into the majors, and Dixie was so much of a southerner that he had even gotten a southern nickname.

But it turned out differently. It turned out that Dixie felt it was a lot more important that the Dodgers play together well and pull together as a team than the fact that one of the players was black. What he told me about hitting to right was basically what I've just described—that getting a base runner from second to third (where he could score on a long fly ball, something he couldn't do from second) meant more to the welfare of the team than my batting average which might drop off a point or two.

It was a minor incident, but I still feel it was important.

I noticed afterwards, too, that as more and more black players came into the major leagues, many southern players would go out of their way to give them advice on the finer points of playing top ball.

Hitting to right isn't simple or easy, once you've gotten to be a fair hitter, but it's by no means impossible. What you have to do is get the bat out in front of the ball and hit toward the right side hole. But you can't wait until you're in a game and try to hit the ball just *hoping* that it will go where you want it to, by some sort of luck. Get your coach or manager to show you how to hold the bat and how to get out in front of the ball.

Just as with bunting, you'll find that after a while you have the trick of hitting to the right. Again, you'll be sacrificing yourself for the good of the team. Sometimes you'll be lucky and find the hole for a base hit, but even if you don't, your manager will remember that you were able to hit the ball the way he wanted you to.

Learning to hit to right, too, will auotmatically mean you're also learning how to deliver on a hit-and-run play whenever the circumstances call for it.

Now, I'd like to close this chapter with a couple of generalizations.

When you're just coming up in the Little Leagues, forget the home run. Just meet the ball, get a hit. "Put the bat on the ball," as Little League coaches are fond of saying.

There was an old-time ball player named Keeler—Wee Willie Keeler, they used to call him, because he was pretty small—who used to come up with some pretty fantastic batting averages. He hit .432 for Baltimore in 1897. He was once asked what the secret of his success was and he said: "I hit 'em where they ain't."

What he meant was that he never tried for distance, he never tried to hit the long ball, he just hit the ball where it was pitched. A lot of pretty fair country ball players have had mighty successful careers in the big leagues doing just that.

Early in your career you should try to find out what kind of hitter you are basically. But you shouldn't try to force it. Maybe you *are* a natural long-ball hitter. If so, so much the better. But if you keep trying for the long ball and keep striking out or popping up, I'd choke up on the bat a little and concentrate for a while on just getting hits.

One thing I found out as a youngster, was that I just wasn't cut out to be a home-run hitter. I was a good hitter, but not a long-ball hitter, and I just faced up to that fact. That's what you must do—what every Little Leaguer must do. Know yourself and your own capabilities.

Once I faced up to that about myself, I concentrated entirely on just meeting the ball squarely and never worrying about how far it was going.

There's a great temptation to forget this when you're under tension because of the circumstances in a game, but you mustn't. I remember very clearly a number of times when I'd be going up to home plate when it would be getting toward the end of the game and we'd be behind a run or two. There would be a man on first or second, and I'd think to myself, boy, I've got to hit the ball out of the park this time.

If you're a natural singles hitter, that kind of thinking is fatal. What you do in that case is to overswing—starting to swing too hard at the top of your swing, as I emphasized earlier—and you spoil the natural rhythm of your swing, pulling you off-balance. Instead of hitting the ball out of the park, all you do is make an out.

Stay with your natural swing and get a hit, no matter how much you want to hit a long ball.

What I used to do when that feeling began coming over me was to step back out of the batter's box and say to myself: Okay, Robinson, be yourself, do what comes naturally, don't overswing, just meet the ball and get yourself a hit, let the next guy go for the long ball.

Oh, I had my share of home runs and long fly balls with men on, but it wasn't the result of deliberately trying for them. Maybe at that particular time I got a little more under the ball and it carried farther, but it was a natural kind of thing. If you're a singles hitter, be a singles hitter. You help your club more that way.

When you step into the batter's box, always remember that your greatest value to your club is to get on base—and it doesn't matter how. Eddie Stanky knew it, and many a time I've watched Stanky foul off, pitch after pitch, until he drew a walk. My greatest asset in the game was my reflexes, my ability to upset the opposing pitcher by my tactics on the bases. There were many times when I felt that just getting on first was more valuable than a home run.

Summary

These are the things you should remember about hitting:

1. *Keep your eye on the ball.*
2. *Stay with your most comfortable stance.*
3. *Develop a smooth, natural swing.*
4. *Hit off your back foot.*
5. *Follow through.*
6. *Learn to bunt and to hit to right.*
7. *Forget the homer, just hit the ball.*

3

●●●●●●●●●●

BASE RUNNING

Little League base running is a good deal simpler than base running in the major leagues, obviously—because of the Little League rule that a runner cannot leave his base until the ball has either been hit or has passed the plate—but there are a few points that a good Little League player should keep in his mind.

1. RUNNING TO FIRST
2. SLIDING
3. BASE STEALING

Running to First

As I said in my introduction, the instant you hit a ball, get down to first at absolutely your top speed, every time. Don't wait to see where the ball went, don't figure that you're a sure out, even if you see the second baseman come up with the ball.

I know in major league ball you'll sometimes see a runner sort of slowing up because he sees the second baseman has the ball and is already throwing to first while he's still halfway down the line. I never approved of that kind of base running. After the first baseman has the ball in his mitt, all right, but even in the major leagues, first basemen have been known to make errors.

In the Little League, however, errors are far more frequent. As the runner, keep in mind that the second base-man may make a wild throw, or that the first baseman may drop the ball.

So, I repeat, on every ball you hit, drive down to first as hard as you can and don't let up till you've stepped on that bag running over it.

Now, if you've hit a ball to the outfield, you shouldn't run straight over the bag. You should be running as hard as you can, but about fifteen or twenty feet from first base you should veer a little to the right, and then round first heading toward second, kicking the base with your left foot. By the time you've gotten twenty feet past first you should be able to pick up the play in the outfield and be able to determine whether you can go on to second. If the ball has gone by the outfielder, you can go on; if he's already firing it back in, you have time to get back to first safely.

Two anecdotes of my own career come to mind, because they both illustrate a major facet of base running I'd like to emphasize: Alertness.

In the 1955 World Series, it appeared that the Dodgers were going to lose to the Yankees again. We had lost the four previous series, and in this fifth series we had lost the first two games.

Before the third game, I decided that I was going to be just as aggressive on the base paths as I knew how. So in one inning I was on first and there was a base hit to left field. I tore down to second and rounded the base, and just as Elston Howard came up with the ball, I slowed down as if to stop. Naturally, Howard threw toward second base be-hind me and just as he let go of the ball, knowing that I had the reflexes to get started again, I went on into third.

I made it easily because the infielder who took the throw from Howard had to hurry his own throw to third, and as a result it was in high. I slid in under it. Players who might have been faster than me, but who couldn't start or stop as well, wouldn't have been able to make that play. Of course, a play like that can backfire on you in the major leagues if your timing isn't right down to the split second, but in this case the whole Dodger team caught fire. We won that game, and three of the next four, and went on to win the series.

In Little League play, with a ball hit on the ground to the left fielder, when you round second, keep your eye like a hawk on that left fielder. If you're fifteen to twenty feet past second, he's likely to hurry his throw. If his throw goes to second right on the mark, you have plenty of time to get back; if he throws to third you can stay where you are till you see whether the third baseman gets it.

My other anecdote concerns Johnny Schmitz, who used to be one of the top pitchers for the Chicago Cubs. Again this emphasizes my point that being alert to what's happening can frequently do as much good for your club as doing something spectacular, like hitting a home run.

For some reason, we Dodgers always had trouble getting runs off Schmitz. I don't know, to this very day, why that was. Johnny was a lefty, and the Dodgers, back in those days, were regarded as a particularly strong right-handed hitting ball club. We were supposed to murder left-handed pitching. But we never did against Johnny. He had a very tantalizing slow curve, and from the same motion he had a fast curve, and by mixing these up he was a very effective pitcher. Usually our games were very close—1-0, 2-1, 3-2. Johnny was very wise in the ways of pitching and, as I said, although we were a very strong hitting team, he used his wisdom to keep us pretty well off-balance.

At any rate, in this particular instance, we had a tie game going as we went into the closing innings, it was either 1-1 or 0-0 as I came up to bat, and I came up to bat with nobody on base.

I worked the count to three-and-two and on the next pitch, Schmitz—who practically always had beautiful control—somehow let the ball get away from him. I saw it, and I also saw, when the ball was about thirty feet from the plate, that it was going to slam into the dirt.

Instead of just tossing my bat aside and trotting down to first, I charged off at top speed and as I looked back I saw that the ball had bounced off the catcher's chest protector, and he was chasing after it. I simply just kept on going, without losing a stride, as fast as I could, and I slid in safely with time to spare. The next batter got a hit, and we went on to win.

It's being alert for things like that that make you the kind of player a manager wants, the kind of player who helps a team. In baseball, you *never* know where the ball is going, whether it's being thrown or being batted. I've seen some of the best players in the majors—and you have, too—throw a ball away or fumble it. If you're playing against a top player, you figure that ninety-nine times out of a hundred the ball is going where he means to throw it. It's that hundredth time that you have to be watching for, every time.

Sliding

In the Little Leagues, sliding is the essence of simplicity. It doesn't require a great deal of practice—you're not in the major leagues where you have to get into the technicalities of how to start your slide, and you don't have to practice hook sliding—but you ought to get in a little practice because there undoubtedly will be games during your season when you will need to slide.

Where you practice is on the grass. Considering the relatively few times during your season that you will slide, there's no sense getting slide burns practicing on the base paths. And you should practice sliding only in sneakers or in baseball shoes with rubber or synthetic cleats, not with real baseball shoes, if you have them. There's no sense in a

Little Leaguer breaking an ankle just trying to learn to slide.

All that you should bother about is coming into the base feet first, on your side, and totally relaxed.

This is where I advise you *not* to take major leaguers as a model for sliding.

In the first place, by the time most major leaguers get up there to play, they've had years of practice and coaching on how to slide. And through years of experience and plenty of hard knocks, they know exactly what they can do and what they can't. They know what can go wrong. And their bodies are far tougher than yours, no matter how good a shape you're in.

So, at the start of your season, just get enough practice so that you learn to slide relaxed, and let it go at that.

Base Stealing

Because of Little League rules, there are very few stolen bases made on wild pitches, wild throws, or passed balls, but there are a number of things that you should keep in mind. The first is that you should take a look at how far the backstop is behind home plate. I've seen them range all the way from fifteen to twenty-four feet. This obviously will have an effect on how fast the catcher can get back to the ball if it gets by him. The closer it is, the more careful you have to be.

As a general rule of thumb, however, you have a pretty good chance of getting from first to second on a wild pitch or a passed ball, and a pretty fair chance of getting home from third. The steal on which I'd be most cautious is trying to get from second to third. If the catcher does come up with the ball and the third baseman is any good, the throw down to him is the shortest the catcher has to make.

When you're on first, however, I have a suggestion for you. Now, the pitcher knows that according to Little

League rules, you can't steal on him. The minute he puts his foot on the rubber, you have to be touching first base. You can't even jump up and down on the base.

I'm one hundred percent in favor of that. It's the duty of every runner at first, no matter what league he's in, to try to worry the pitcher. And even in the Little League you can disturb a pitcher's concentration, especially in a tight situation, by jumping to a lead off first and then jumping back a few times. You may even be able to disturb his concentration enough so that his next pitch will be a ball instead of a strike.

But I suggest that, if you're serious about baseball—and I assume that you are—that you go even a step further in your own mind and start figuring out when you're on first what you *would* do if you *could* steal. Start figuring out just how much of a lead you think you could get on the pitcher, and try going out that far a couple of times.

When I was on the Dodgers, I used to watch Peewee Reese marking off a line in the dirt of the base path as a reference mark to show him how much of a lead he might get on a pitcher and still be able to get back to first safely if the pitcher threw over.

You could even try that out for yourself while you're still in Little League, though not many players in the majors do it. I never did it myself.

But Reese, like all other major leaguers, was forever testing out the pitchers. In addition to that, Reese knew his own abilities down to the finest detail, and what was just as important, he knew what he could do with them.

He was a thinking ballplayer, and it's the player who thinks, who knows what he can do and who figures out in advance just exactly what he is going to do, who makes the real base stealer.

As I said, I never drew a line in the dirt of the base path the way Reese did, but I always had my lead figured out,

whether I was going to steal or whether I was just trying to
bother the pitcher.

As a matter of fact back in my playing days, I always
used to take a bigger lead off first when I wasn't going to
steal, than when I was really ready to go.

There was a basic reason for this.

When I didn't really intend to steal, I knew when the
pitcher started his motion I had only one way to go, and
that was back to the base. Whether he was actually going to
pitch to the batter or throw to first didn't matter, I would
already be leaning back toward the bag. That would make
it pretty sure, if I had my big lead and the pitcher threw to
first, that I could get back safely.

On the other hand, if I really was going to try to steal
second, I couldn't take as big a lead; because when the
pitcher started his motion, I wanted to be leaning toward
second, not back toward first.

This was so that I could start for second the instant he
started to throw, as fast and as hard as I could, hoping that
I'd figured out his motion.

When you're really going to steal, every fraction of a second counts. In the majors, or in any kind of organized ball,
the difference between *safe* and *out* is a matter of fractions.
The knowledge you have, and the way you use that knowledge, is more often than not the difference. You can be dar-
ing, but you also must use the knowledge that you've
learned.

Part of this learning—in fact, the first and biggest part of
it—is knowing yourself. Know how much a lead you can
take and still get back safely to first; know how much of a
lead you need to get in order to be able to make a steal.
When you get to the Babe Ruth League, or high school,
where you can steal, make a practice of getting far enough
off base so that the pitcher has to throw to first, time and
again. It will teach you how much of a lead you can take,

and it will show you the moves of the pitcher. If he can't nail you when you have a two-step lead, try three steps.

When I was in the big leagues, I knew that when I was on first, my job was to make the pitcher worry on every pitch that I might be going to second. Even when I was a youngster I was a good base stealer, so I always represented a threat. Even when I wasn't going to try to steal second, I could still worry the pitcher enough so that he couldn't concentrate one hundred per cent on throwing to the batter. He had to have in the back of his mind that I might possibly be going on the next pitch, which might make him just a little bit less effective when he made his delivery.

There are only two further generalizations I want to make on stealing in general.

Base stealing, with the possible exception of hitting, is a matter of reflexes more than anything else in baseball. I don't care how fast a man is, he isn't necessarily a good base stealer. I remember all the times I've watched Maury Wills. It seems to me Wills had such terrific reflexes that when he started to steal, by the time he had taken two or three strides, he would be going at top speed. And how he could fly!

In addition to that, of course, he knew every move in the game, and he knew every move of almost every opposing pitcher.

Wills or any other great base stealer doesn't get that way just because of his speed and reflexes—he has to know the opposing pitchers, too. That's why I want you to get into the habit of studying pitchers when you're on base in the Little League. Not just watching, studying. It might even help you with your hitting. Many Little League pitchers have slightly different moves depending on whether they're throwing a fast ball or a curve or a change-up. See if you can spot the differences.

And if you can spot the difference, pass it on to your teammates. That's one advantage of being on a team. You don't have to do everything yourself. All the players on a Little League team should be trying to help each other.

My final comment is that, in base stealing, you steal on the pitcher, not the catcher.

In the major leagues, any catcher playing regularly has to have an arm strong enough so that you can't steal on him provided he gets the ball in time. The man you have to beat, the man you get the lead on, is the pitcher.

When a runner knows the pitcher, he knows how to get that little extra half-step lead. If you study a pitcher hard enough, you'll see there's something in his delivery, some slight change in his motions somewhere along the line, that will give you a tip-off on whether he's going to first base or whether he's going home.

Of course the pitchers know this too, and they spend hours practicing their pick-off moves. Like everyone else, they get better with practice and they know how to cover up —the really great ones like Warren Spahn are terrific at this —and yet if you are really observant and you study pitchers carefully, you'll find that most of them really do have certain different little moves depending on where they're going.

You ought to know what's going through the catcher's mind, too, at that time. He knows subconsciously that if you're a good base runner and you go, it means you figured you had enough of a lead to make the steal attempt work. This knowledge will make even the best catchers tend to hurry their throw, with the result that maybe the throw will be just a little off target—giving you that little extra edge which may be all you need.

Roy Campanella of the Dodgers was one of the best catchers there was in baseball and he had one of the strongest arms ever, but I've even seen him forced to hurry his throw.

Summary

Here is what you should concentrate on in base running:

1. *Run out* every *hit.*
2. *Be alert.*
3. *Learn to slide.*
4. *Worry the pitcher.*
5. *Round first on outfield hits.*

4

●●●●●●●●●●

INFIELD PLAY

I would estimate that possibly ninety percent of the action in a baseball game takes place in the infield, and certainly all of the fast action takes place there. Trying to explain infield play is so complicated that I've broken it down into a number of categories:

1. THE BASICS
2. THE DOUBLE PLAY
3. THE SHORTSTOP
4. SECOND BASE
5. FIRST BASE
6. THIRD BASE

The Basics

With the possible exception of the catcher, major league infielders have the greatest physical demands put on them. They must be able to start like jackrabbits to get a jump on the ball; they must be able to get off a hard snap throw while running at full speed; they must be able to throw while in the air—a shortstop jumping up to avoid a runner at second while throwing to first is the example I have in mind—they must be able to throw while kneeling down or running bent over. In other words, they must have legs like

51

steel springs and arms like whipcord and be in top physical condition all around.

Here are some general rules that apply to all infielders:

1. If you possibly can, move over to get in front of a ground ball. If you reach for a ball with your glove, when it's off to one side, and you miss it, it's gone into the outfield. If you have your body in front of it and you can't field it cleanly—say it takes an unexpected hop—at least you've got it trapped. And that's a cardinal rule for infielders: If you can't field a ball cleanly, trap it.

2. Go down by bending your knees, if you possibly can. Don't bend over from your waist. If a ball is coming straight at you on the ground, for example, don't bend forward from your waist and put your hands down; bend your knees so that your body is only leaning forward a slight bit.

3. Keep your hands relaxed, and keep your glove below the level of the ball. If your glove hand, especially, is tense, the ball may jump out of your glove. And the reason for keeping your glove low is twofold. First, most balls that get through an infielder go below his glove. Second, if your glove is too high and the ball takes a bad hop, your glove will block the ball out of your line of vision. It's easier to follow a ball that comes up than one that dips. In other words, if you've got your knees fully bent and your glove is almost at ground level and the ball comes up, you know exactly where it is. If you're bent over, and your glove is about level with your knees and the ball dips down, you've got a great chance of losing it.

I still remember watching Eddie Miller when he was playing for the Cincinnati Reds, years and years ago. Eddie

FIELDING GROUNDERS

KNEES
BENT

HANDS
RELAXED
BELOW LEVEL
OF THE BALL

FIELDING GROUNDERS / Get in front of the ball to trap it; go down by bending your knees, hands relaxed, glove below the level of the ball.

was one of the best fielding shortstops of all times and almost every time he went down for a ground ball, it seemed to me he would come up with a handful of dirt as well as the ball—as if to keep reminding himself to keep his hands down real low fielding those ground balls.

Maybe that wouldn't be such a bad thing to try yourself as a Little League infielder.

When you've gotten those basics down, you still have a lot to learn. You've got to learn what you should do when a fly ball is hit to the outfield (depending on where it's hit in the outfield), where you go to be in position for cut-off throws. Now, almost every Little League coach has his own way of teaching you where he wants you to play, so I'm not going to go into detail on this. I simply want to emphasize that if you're a shortstop and a ball is hit into left field, the play hasn't ended. You should be on your way to a designated position, depending on the circumstances at the time.

You'll also have to learn to take into account the situation of the game on every single given play—not the situation on the play before. You have to take into account what you should do if there is no runner on base, if there's a runner on first or second, if there are no outs, or one out—and so on.

Here again concentration is vitally important because if an infielder forgets how many outs there are—and I've seen major league infielders lose track of outs because their concentration had been distracted by a rhubarb on the field or something—he can make a wrong play that might let a run score when he could have cut it off.

Of course, as you get older and more experienced, and if you keep studying the game and the players the way I think you should, you'll get to know not only where to play for a right-handed batter or a lefty, you'll even get to know how to play individual batters.

I remember a crucial game we were playing against the

Giants. Carl Erskine was pitching for us and Willie Mays was the batter. I knew the kind of pitcher Erskine was, and I knew the kind of hitter Mays was, so I moved a step or two to my left. When Willie hit a line drive, I was able to stab it, taking an almost sure hit away from Willie. The reason I remember it so clearly is that it saved a no-hitter for Erskine: But I mention it only to emphasize how you as a player not only have to concentrate on every play, but on every pitch.

You can't just figure where you should be playing generally and stay there, you have to figure out where you should be playing every time the pitcher throws the ball. Of course, in the majors, you have to be a little bit subtle about your moves. You can't be so obvious as to tip off the opposing team, because they watch the position of the infielders —and the outfielders—all the time. The opposing hitters, especially, watch the positioning of the fielders like hawks; because this may give them a tip-off on what kind of pitch to expect.

Even in the short Little League season, by the time it's half over, you should have a mental book on the hitters of the opposing team and be able to position yourself accordingly.

I'd like to give just one final example, where the kind of thinking I'm talking about paid off in my career.

We were in Philadelphia for the last game of the 1951 season. Don Newcombe was pitching for us, Eddie Waitkus was the hitter, the bases were loaded and there were two outs in an extra-inning ball game. Don was pitching well at the time. He was an overpowering fast-ball thrower, and he was throwing hard. I knew the kind of hitter Eddie was, a line-drive hitter, not so much a pull hitter. He would hit the ball where it was thrown. I figured that since Don's fast ball was going so well, this was what he would throw, so I moved a step toward second base, figuring that if Eddie hit the ball, he would hit it straightaway.

This little move paid off. Eddie hit a line drive that would have gone into center field to win the ball game, except that I was near enough to dive and get the ball. So the game went into another inning and we were able to win and go into a play-off with the Giants for the National League pennant.

It was because I knew the kind of pitcher Don Newcombe was and I knew the kind of hitter Eddie Waitkus was and I could make a pretty good guess as to where the ball was most likely to go. Of course, you can guess wrong, too. In baseball, you never can be positive where the ball is going until it's been hit, but in a tight situation, you should always play the percentages. That goes for Little League, too.

The Double Play

The double play is one of the fastest plays in baseball, and by all odds it's the most important play that can be made in the infield. It's also the one that requires the most coordination between the infielders, and the one that requires the most practice. And it's the most difficult play that an infielder can be called upon to make.

To me the prettiest play in all of baseball is the three-six-three double play, first baseman to shortstop back to first. To make that play, the first baseman has to get the ball fast, he has to get his throw away fast—making sure he doesn't hit the runner with the ball—and he has to get over to first base fast, because by the time he gets there, the ball will already be half-way back.

While I'd like to go further into the fine points of the double play as the professionals do it, so that you can appreciate what you're seeing when it's really well-executed, I'll confine myself to the Little League play at the start.

The first thing I'd like to emphasize is that, to start a double play, a fielder must first have the ball. That may sound a little silly, but I've seen many errors in Little League play because a shortstop was so anxious to get a double play that he started throwing to second before he had the ball.

Strangely enough, this occurs more frequently with infielders who've had a little experience playing than with ten-year-olds just starting out. The ten-year-old isn't worrying about a double play, he's having enough trouble fielding the ball.

The second thing in the double play: Once the infielder is *positive* he has the ball in his hand, he's to throw to second —accurately. Again this may sound silly, but I've seen it happen. Again it's because the fielder is so anxious to double-up that he throws off-target.

So the second rule of the double play in Little League is, *make sure you get the man out at second.* Then, even if the double play isn't completed, at least you have one out.

It is here that the play gets a little complicated, because the infielder covering second has his work cut out for him. There are four separate things that he *must* do.

1. *Catch the throw.*
2. *Tag second.*
3. *Get out of the way of the runner coming down from first.*
4. *Throw hard and accurately down to first.*

I think that if a youngster can learn to do all that by the time he's too old to play in the Little League, he's done an excellent job of learning the basics of the double play.

The key to making the double play in Little League is not to get rattled. Concentrate absolutely on what you're doing, one step at a time. If the man fielding the ball flubs it, there goes the whole play right there. If he throws wild, there it goes again. Similarly, if the man covering second either drops the throw or doesn't touch the bag—and at this point we're still taking about getting the man out at second.

Assuming that we get that man out, the infielder covering second—and it has to be either the shortstop or the second baseman, more likely the latter—then has to get out of the way of the base runner because the runner's idea, once he sees he's out, is to try to hit the fielder to see if he can make him drop the ball.

Then comes the throw to first, and that's where the infielder's practice in throwing is put to its toughest test. On a simple ground ball to the infield with no runner on base, the throw to first has to be hard and accurate, but normally the fielder has a second or so to get himself set and make sure of what he's doing.

In the actual double play, *nobody* has a chance to get set. The man who fields the ball has to make a snap throw as quick and as hard as he can. The man covering second has to be set for it, get it, then turn and fire as quick and as hard as *he* can down to first base.

All that comes with time. However, in Little League, follow the steps I've outlined, one by one, practicing them as much as you can, making sure that you've gotten each step down perfectly before you move on to the next.

Of all the double-play combinations you will come up against, the one that requires incessant practice is the shortstop-second baseman play.

When I was on the Dodgers, I was an All-Star second baseman and Peewee Reese was an All-Star shortstop. The thing that made us a really good double-play combination was that we'd go out on the field and practice our moves and our throws until we got to know what each other was doing, down to the last fine detail.

This, let me emphasize, was when we were both All-Stars. But to go on being an All-Star, you have to be as close to perfect as you can get, and the only way to achieve that is to keep on practicing. You might as well face up to it early. Even when you get to be an All-Star, you go out the next day and practice. So we'd get a fungo hitter and he'd keep hitting to Reese and Reese would come up with the ball and throw to me at second, and I'd make my move to first. Then vice-versa.

The reason for all the practice is that if you make double plays only in actual games, you may have a long streak of double plays that are all basically the same, and all of a sudden a totally different one comes up. If you've just been playing in games, you're rusty on it. With a fungo hitter, he can place the ball differently on every hit, and the double play combination has to work differently on all those hits.

Through all this practice, Reese would know where I would head for no matter where the ball was hit toward him, so he could throw to a certain position. Only experience teaches you how to make these plays, but the basic thing is that the shortstop never throws to where his teammate is, he throws to a position where his teammate is going to be. The shortstop has to learn to throw to this position on all types of balls, and the second baseman has to know what position he's throwing to so that he can get over there and get the ball.

You can't play this sort of refined ball in Little League, but you ought to have it in the back of your mind as what you want to work up to.

The Shortstop

Sometimes I think shortstop is the most difficult of all positions to play in baseball.

I mentioned about all infielders having to be able to get jack-rabbit starts and throw from almost any position and be able to make snap-throws with something on the ball, but these demands are made most heavily—or most frequently—on the shortstop.

Most good ball players have good arms, but the demands on infielders' arms are different from those made on outfielders . An outfielder can rear back and get the full

SHORT STOP

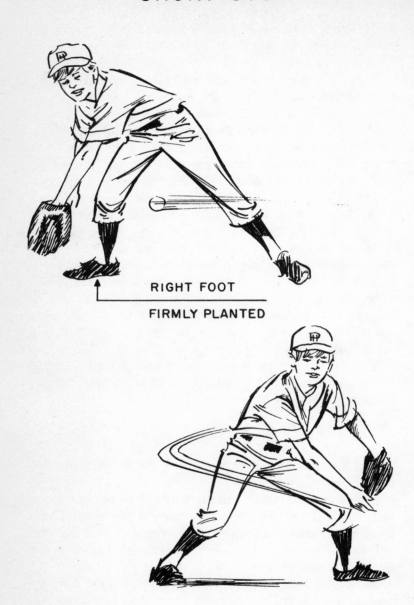

RIGHT FOOT
FIRMLY PLANTED

SHORTSTOP: FIELDING/ Plant right foot hard the instant you catch the ball. Memorize position at first where you must throw and be able to do it from all positions.

strength of his body behind his throw, an infielder has to make snap throws most of the time, throwing the ball just with his arm. A shortstop can't waste any time getting set.

He has to learn to get rid of the ball fast, and with all he can get on it.

He must be able to go into the hole and still get enough on the ball to get the runner out at first; he must be able to go behind second, and again get enough on the ball.

The basic of getting enough on your throw is to get that right foot planted, hard, the instant you catch the ball. The instant after, not the instant before.

You can practice shortstop fielding—as you can any fielding—right in your own back yard. All you need is your glove, a ball, a bat, and a fungo hitter. To build up your alertness, have the ball hit so that it isn't where you want it —off to your left, to your right, hard at you, dribblers. Practice throwing off-balance as much as you can—it's a trick you learn only through practice.

It's always better to throw from a set position, obviously, and only playing will teach you when you have the time to get set, because so many variables enter into it—the speed of the batted ball, the speed of the runner, the length of the throw. But there are a lot of times when you just have to come up throwing.

Take, for example, the ball that is just barely hit past the pitcher. You have to come charging in to get it, and if it has been hit off to one side, you have to throw from a position where you're bent over and running. If you don't get rid of the ball fast, the runner will be safe.

For a couple of years on the Dodgers I watched Peewee Reese make some of the most fantastic plays I've ever seen. I finally decided that the real basis of his success was that he had such a terrific snap throw, hard, fast, and low.

Another thing you ought to do when you're practicing is to have a certain number of hard ground balls hit directly to you. That kind of ball can be the most difficult ball of all to field for the reason that it's far more difficult to gauge its hop. On a ball that's hit to one side or the other, you have two lines of sight on it so that you can see more clearly its line of flight, but on a ball hit directly to you, you have only one line of sight. In other words, if a ball is hit a little to one side you can see how sharply it's dipping down, so you can gauge how it's going to bounce up. You can't do that when it's coming directly at you.

Once you master the techniques of fielding and throwing at shortstop, playing the position should begin to come easier. Even a play like the double-play ball is not so difficult because there are only a limited number of things that you can do.

If you field a double-play ball on the third base side of your position, you know you won't be able to get to second in time to complete the play, so you throw to the second baseman covering the bag. There may be rare occasions when the ball is hit past the pitcher so close to second that you can field it, tag second yourself and then throw to first.

A word of caution on that. Just tag second and cross it, don't stand there to throw. If you do, that runner coming down from first will try to carry you right on out to center field.

Again, I used to watch Peewee Reese make that play, going across second. Sometimes he'd just flick the bag with his right foot, his momentum carrying him a couple of steps out of the runner's way before he'd jam on his right foot to make his throw. That's when he had a little time, maybe half a second. Other times he'd hit the base and use it to stop himself, and jump straight up in the air to avoid the runner and make his throw to first while he was actually in the air—like a jump pass by a football quarterback. Still other times, when he had the time, he'd stop himself with the base and back off a step toward left field to make his throw.

These were all variants of the same basic play. Reese

knew what he had to do, and he knew what he could do, and the reason he did it so well was that he worked so hard at it.

I'd like to make a point about how you throw from second to first on the double play. If you're at second base, you throw the ball straight down the base line, and throw it head high. The purpose of that is not to hit the runner, he knows you're going to throw. It's to make him start his slide a fraction of a second before he wants to.

You have to respect that runner coming down at full speed from first base. What he wants to do is hit the fielder, whether it's the shortstop or the second baseman, in order to break up the double play, and he'll hit you if he can. What you have to do is make those base runners respect you. If you don't, they'll run right over you every time. The base runner has his eye on the ball too, you know. If he sees the ball coming toward him, he knows it's up to him to get out of the way. The minute you start to throw, he'll be thinking about getting out of the way.

There's another advantage to that kind of throw. Besides making the runner start his slide earlier than he wants, it gives you an extra fraction of a second to get out of the way when he comes jamming into the bag.

Second Base

This is the position in baseball that I came to like the best and that I played the most.

When I first came up to the Montreal ball club in the Dodgers' farm, I'd never played second base. I didn't have the faintest idea how to play the position. Not only was I unable to make the moves, I didn't even know what the moves were. As for making the double play, all I knew was what I'd seen watching them, which was practically nothing.

Fortunately, there was a guy on the club who believed in

the kind of team-work that I talked about earlier, a guy named Lou Rochelle. Rochelle believed in helping his teammates, even green kids who had just come up. I don't know how much time he spent with me, positioning me around second base for all sorts of different plays, teaching me the different ways of making the double play.

I developed three basic moves for my way of making the double play at second.

If the ball was hit to the left side of the infield, the instant I saw it, I'd race for second to take the throw. Then came one of the three basic moves:

1. I'd take the throw going across the bag, kick the bag with my left foot, plant my right foot and pivot for the throw to first.

2. Or, I'd fake with my body as if I were going across—to get the runner to commit himself to sliding on the infield side of the bag to try to break up the play—then I'd back off to make my throw.

3. I'd take the throw and take a step toward left field to make the throw.

The reason for all that is if you have a different number of ways of making the plays, you can put a question into the base runner's mind as to what you're going to do. His main idea is to hit you to break up the play, but if he doesn't know where you're going to be, it makes it all the harder.

If you have only one way of making the play, the runner has a much greater chance of breaking it up.

At the very first, in the Little League, all you should worry about, whether you're the second baseman or the shortstop, is getting the runner out at second. Even on that play, you'll find if you don't move out of the base runner's way, he'll bang into you just to see if he can make you drop the ball. But even in Little League, after you've gotten the

KEEPING YOUR EYE ON THE BALL   I just made a solid hit to right;
notice how my eye is still on the ball. The picture also illustrates
what I've said about keeping your rear foot (my right foot)
locked firmly in place. Even though the momentum of my follow-
through has pulled my right heel off the ground, my spikes are
still dug in where I had them when I started my swing. (UPI)

A MODEL BUNT   I just laid one down the third base line and the catcher is getting rid of his mask to go after it. (He didn't get it in time.) Note how far back my bat is. In bunting, never reach out to meet the ball, as I've emphasized. Just let the ball come in and hit the bat. (UPI)

SCRAMBLING BACK TO FIRST   A lesson for Little Leaguers is "alertness." I just made it back to first after trying to steal second in a game against the Cubs. Note how I was able to get into the bag by sliding under the first baseman's arm. (UPI)

THE WAY TO SLIDE   In this play I could see from the catcher's stance that the ball was shoulder high . . .

. . . This allowed me to slide in under and away from the tag, going into a scissors split and kicking up a lot of dust . . .

. . . The umpire is calling me safe. When you're base running, watching the catcher (or whatever opposing baseman may be involved) tells you where the ball is. (UPI)

THE CLASSIC DOUBLE PLAY

(1) I field the ball and make a snap throw to Peewee Reese who is just coming up on second.

(2) Reese kicks second with his left foot.

(3) Reese starts his jump to get out of the way of the runner's spikes.

(4) High in the air, Reese starts his throw.

(5) Reese releases the ball.

(6) Reese is coming down, the ball on its way to first, his momentum carrying him clear of the runner. (UPI)

This sequence illustrates perfect timing gained by practice and an all-important point for Little Leaguers: Make sure of the out at second before worrying about the runner going to first.

IN A JAM Here's the kind of situation you can get yourself into if you don't keep your eyes open. I was tagged out. (UPI)

SECOND BASE

PIVOT FOOT

MOVE TO FORCE RUNNER
TO INFIELD SIDE

STEP OR
TWO TO THE RIGHT

SECOND BASE: (*Three Ways of Making Double Play When Ball is Hit to Left*) (1) Take throw going across bag, kick bag with left foot, plant right foot and pivot for throw to first. (2) Fake a move to cross the bag and force the runner to slide on infield side, then back off for throw. (3) Receive throw and take a step or two to right field to make throw.

runner out, you should look to see if you have a chance of making the play at first.

In these beginning days, there's no harm in practicing the three ways I listed of making the play at second. It gives you experience with different moves so that you're not always doing the same thing the same way.

If you figure out a different way to make the play, go right ahead. But I don't think that you really need more than three basic ways of doing it. Trying to figure out too many fancy ways of doing something doesn't pay off in the end.

I have a word of caution about trying for the double play, especially in the Little League, and that's getting to know whether you should throw to first at all. I've even seen major leaguers throw to first when there wasn't a prayer of making the play, and you don't have a major leaguer playing first base for you. If you have a doubt in your mind, don't throw. If you try to rush your throw, there's always the danger that it will go wild. You already have one out, the man at second. Sure, the batter is safe at first, but a man on first cannot score on a single. If you make a wild throw and he goes on to second, then he *can* score on a single.

I talked about Lou Rochelle positioning me at second base, telling me where I should be on different play possibilities, how I should play various hitters.

Position is especially important on a double-play possibility. With a man on first and either one out or none, you have to cheat a little on where you position yourself. Instead of playing straightaway second, the way you'd do if there were no man on first, you have to position yourself differently.

What you have to do is move in a little more toward home plate, and move about a step closer to second base. This means a wider gap between you and the first baseman, but you have to take that chance. It's simply playing the odds of the game. No batter can hit precisely where he wants to, no batter can deliberately take advantage of that wider gap—though it's true, if he's lucky, he may hit through—but a chance for a double play is more important. Always play the odds, always go for the double play when the circumstances set up the possibility.

The shortstop, too, has to cheat a little on a possible double play. He has to play a little closer to home plate, and he has to fade a little to the right or the left, depending on where he figures the ball is going to be hit. Again, it's one of the chances you have to take.

I still remember one occasion when my faking probably saved me from a possible spiking on a double-play ball.

We were playing against the then Boston Braves, before they moved, first to Milwaukee, then to their present city, Atlanta.

The first baseman for the Braves then was Earl Torgeson, a tough, competitive player. Torgie was the runner on first. The instant the ball was hit to the left side of the infield, I started for second; Torgie already charging down the baseline, set on breaking up the play. He probably could see that he was already out, but he didn't want me to get the man at first. I gave him a fake on the play as he was starting his slide.

I know he didn't plan it that way, but as he slid into second his legs were so high that one of his shoulders was on the ground and one of his feet hit me on the shoulder. I'm sure that if I hadn't faked he would have had a better shot at me, and I might have been spiked. As it was, Torgie cracked his own shoulder blade as he was sliding along. As I say, I know he wasn't aiming at me, it was just the momentum of his going into his slide that carried his legs up so high. It's things like this you have to remember when you're practicing your faking.

I know it doesn't happen in Little League, but in the majors you'll see some runners come in like a blocking back in football trying to take you out of a play. They'll actually try to throw a body block on you, like a blocking back leading a runner through the opposing backfield. Some come sliding in with their spikes high. All this is part of the rough-and-tumble around second base, it's all part of the game, it just means that you always have to be prepared for anything.

I myself once went into second with a half-slide. It happened in the very first World Series that I ever played in. It was unintentional, of course, as it generally is.

We were playing the Yankees. I was on first and a double-play ball was hit to Phil Rizzuto, the Yankee shortstop. When I saw where the ball was hit, I figured Phil would flip to the second baseman who had started over to cover the bag, so I turned my eyes to the second baseman. When he *didn't* cover the bag, I just went in standing up. What I didn't realize was that Rizzuto had kept the ball and was making the play at second by himself. I barreled straight into him.

If the Yankee players had thought that I had done it deliberately there might have been trouble because Rizzuto was pretty popular with his teammates. Everyone in the ball park, however, including the Yankees, had seen that I just wasn't looking at him.

First Base

A professional first baseman must be an exceptional fielder with a wide range. And he must know that range, because he must be able to decide in a flash, on a ground ball hit between himself and the second baseman, which one of them should get it. It's always better to let the second baseman get it, because if the first baseman has to make the play, he not only has to get the ball, he's also faced with the always-difficult throw to the pitcher covering first.

Now, a Little League first baseman never wanders as far afield as a professional, but there are times when the ball is hit in such a way that he knows he can get it and prevent it

FIRST BASE

LEFT FOOT SET
WIDE STRETCH

FIRST BASE: FIELDING A BALL HIT TO LEFT/ Run to the bag, straddle it. If throw is on home side of base, set your right foot on the bag and stretch as far left as necessary; if on the right field side, set your left foot for your stretch.

from going on into right field, and then he's presented with the same problem as the professional—tossing to the pitcher covering first.

That, therefore, is a maneuver that a Little League first baseman ought to work at if he wants to progress in baseball. Work at cutting off the ball, then tossing. The best way to do it is to be moving toward the moving pitcher—that makes it easier for you to judge where to aim the ball. You have to judge the pitcher's speed, and you should keep the throw chest high so that the pitcher doesn't have to bend over to get the ball while he's running.

Even in the Little League, once you've gotten past the beginner's stage and you're playing eight or ten feet from the bag, if a ball is hit to left you should practice running to the bag as hard as you can—not trotting. Trotting gets you into bad habits for your future play.

Once at the bag, straddle it. That way you can hold the bag with your right foot if the throw is on the home side of first, and with your left foot if it's on the right field side of first. On a ball hit to the left side, don't bother trying to make up your mind whether the third baseman or the shortstop will be able to field it. Just get over to where you belong fast, so that if a throw comes in, you'll be ready to take it.

You straddle the bag, basically for two reasons. One is that your body provides a target for the man who's fielding the ball to throw at, and the other is that it will give you an opportunity to make your best stretch if the throw is a little off.

If the throw is off on the home side of the base, set your right foot on the edge of the bag and stretch as far left as you have to—or you can. If the throw is to the right field side, set your left foot at the edge of the bag for your stretch.

To become a top first baseman, you have to develop

TOO MUCH SPACE

THIRD BASE

GOOD INTERVAL

THIRD BASE: FIELDING/ Play close enough to the third base line to keep hits from going through the hole for extra bases.

speed and flexibility, because of the amount of stretching you have to do.

I can't count the number of times that Gil Hodges, when he was playing first for the Brooklyn Dodgers, saved his other infielders from errors because he knew how to move and stretch; he was always relaxed. When a ball was thrown a little off-target, Gil was ready to get it.

You really have to be a top athlete to play first. If you watch a really good first baseman in action, at times you'll see he's actually in a split. One foot is anchored to the bag, his other foot the whole way out, leaning over as far as he can, his glove extended the full length.

Nobody expects that kind of performance from a Little Leaguer. To do it without pulling a leg muscle requires plenty of time given to calisthenics, practicing splits a little at a time, at first, then working up to where you can do almost a full split without any trouble at all.

As you progress through the Little League and have the ability and assurance to play a little farther from the bag you should be learning that positioning yourself is just as important to a first baseman as it is to the second baseman or the shortstop. You have to learn whether to position yourself closer toward the line or more toward second base, whether to be playing back against the grass or in a little bit. Obviously, you position yourself differently for a right-handed hitter than a left-handed one, but exactly where to position yourself comes only with experience.

Third Base

Of all the infield positions, the third baseman has the least ground to cover, but he has one vitally important function—to guard that third base line. This is not to say that there have not been great men at third in baseball history (the name of Hall-of-Famer Harold (Pie) Traynor instantly comes to mind), men whose range and quickness would do credit to any infielder. But even if you play third and you do have great range, you are restricted by that vital function that is your first responsibility.

The reason is obvious. When a right-handed pull hitter is up, or a left-hander who is a notorious push-ball hitter, and the ball gets through between the third baseman and the left field line, it is a certain two bases and a possible third. And since the line is off to his right, third basemen probably make more back-handed stabs of the ball than any other player on the field.

Most major league third basemen know almost to the inch just how far away from that third base line they can play, even allowing for a full-length diving stab at the ball.

In Little League, you needn't worry about that. In Little League, just play close enough to the line to make sure that a ball can't get through for extra bases.

Another essential for a third baseman is a quick arm, especially in the Little League since his throws are, on the average, longer than those of any other infielder. It's a simple matter of arithmetic. The Little League shortstop plays in closer to home plate than the shortstop in higher leagues. The third baseman is just that much farther away from first base.

It's not for nothing, however, that third base is called the "hot corner" and as someone once said, "a third baseman plays the ball in self defense if for no other reason." Some of those line drives come off the bats of right-handed power hitters as if they had been shot out of a rifle, and if the third baseman isn't on his toes, knees bent and tensed ready to jump, they go right by him.

Or, if they're hit directly at him, he has to have the quick hands to get the glove up and catch that ball before it hits him.

Tied as he is to the third base line, the third baseman doesn't have to give as much consideration to his positioning as the other infielders, because he doesn't have all the options they do. He may play in or back, but he can't move too far to his left, even when there's a left-handed pull hitter up. In the first place, a left-handed pull hitter is extremely unlikely to hit a ball anywhere near third, but if by some fluke he should, there's always that one-in-a-thousand chance, if the third baseman *had* moved to his left, that the ball would get through the hole between him and the baseline.

And, for third basemen, that is the first sin of all.

Summary

Points about infield play:

1. *Get in front of the ball if possible.*
2. *Block the ball if necessary.*
3. *Bend with your knees.*
4. *Stay relaxed.*
5. *Keep the glove below the ball.*
6. *Play the batters.*
7. *Learn the snap throw.*
8. *On the double play, first make sure of the out at second.*

5

●●●●●●●●●●●●●●●●●●●●●●

PITCHING AND CATCHING

I think that pitching is seventy-five to eighty percent of the ball game, and that next to the pitcher, the catcher occupies the most vital position on the ball field. For that reason I've divided this chapter into two parts as follows:

THE PITCHER

1. CONDITIONING AND THE CURVE BALL
2. THE DELIVERY
3. KEEP YOUR EYE ON THE MITT

THE CATCHER

1. THE FIELD DIRECTOR AND CONDITIONING
2. THE POP-UP
3. THE THROW TO SECOND

Conditioning and the Curve Ball

If pitching is at least seventy-five percent of the game, conditioning is at least seventy-five percent of pitching. You won't be able to do justice to your pitching if you consistently stay up late nights watching television. (I also personally happen to feel that watching too much television doesn't do your eyes any good.)

At your age in the Little League you don't have to work to get into condition the way a professional athlete does, but you might take note of the fact that in the majors, in Spring training, the pitchers—at least, the good ones—are gluttons for training: running, doing calisthenics, building the strength of their arms and legs and body.

I think that youngsters in the Little League today recognize the importance of condition, by and large, certainly more so than most youngsters when I was growing up. I think they know their bodies have to be in top shape to play the best ball that they are capable of. And the youngsters of today, I think, are bigger and stronger, on the average, than the youngsters of only a generation ago. This, together with the fact that Little League managers and coaches recognize the value of getting their players into shape at the very start of the season, prevents more players from getting injured than in former days.

I agree with the reasoning of the Little League itself, and of almost all Little League managers, that their pitchers shouldn't be allowed to throw curve balls, because in that age bracket, throwing curves is almost certain to hurt your arm. The arm just isn't strong enough yet—a curve, or throwing curves steadily—takes more out of your arm than you might think.

Even if a young pitcher sticks to throwing fast balls and change-ups, however, he can also hurt his arm by throwing too hard at the start of the season's practice, when he hasn't been throwing for months, maybe. Even when a young pitcher *is* in condition, he can hurt himself trying to throw too hard before he's "warmed up." I've seen even seasoned major league pitchers do that very thing.

As a matter of fact, this applies to infielders and even to outfielders. Every player has to get into condition, and once in condition, he has to get warmed up before every game, no matter what his position. A smart player is the one who begins by just loosening the muscles in his arm by tossing

PITCHING CONTROL

HIGH

LOW

IN   OR   OUT

PITCHING: CONTROL / Using your natural motion, imagine there's a catcher's mitt where you're trying to throw, high or low, in or out.

the ball at first and then gradually throwing harder and harder until finally he feels that he can really cut loose and burn the ball in. But, I emphasize, this must be done gradually. Take plenty of time!

There's another item I'd like to touch on in the matter of pitching, and that's the windup. Major league pitchers use the windup to give them more power, to get more speed on their pitches.

The reason Little League Pitchers don't use a windup is that their problem isn't power or speed. It's control.

A youngster who wants to be a good Little League pitcher must first of all get his control under his command, for that is the essential factor in all pitching. I don't care how hard you throw, if you can't control your pitches, you can't be effective.

Take the case of Sandy Koufax. At his retirement in 1966, he was baseball's top pitcher. In that year, for example he led both major leagues in five categories—the lowest earned run average (1.73), most victories (27), most strikeouts (317), most innings pitched (323) and most complete games (27). With a record like that, you'd say that Sandy was close to being a perfect pitcher, but it hadn't always been that way. Until he mastered his control, he had never been a big winner, even though everybody in baseball knew that he was one of the hardest throwers who ever walked out to a pitcher's mound.

Fast-ball pitchers do very well in the Little Leagues, generally on their speed alone. That's partly because the Little League pitcher tends to be the biggest and strongest player on the team. But even in Little League a top pitcher should develop another pitch, a change-up. That should be enough in Little League.

Later on, of course, a pitcher has to develop a variety of pitches, starting with a curve. I don't recommend trying to develop a curve in Little League. As doctors explain it, all the muscles that control your hand action when you're throwing a ball are hinged at the inside of your elbow. Throwing a fast ball puts a certain amount of strain on those muscles, but throwing a curve puts much more of a strain on them, which you should avoid at your age. The danger of hurting your arm is just too great.

As a matter of fact, I don't think that you should fool around trying to develop any sort of fancy pitches while you're still in Little League.

The basic thing you should strive for, with proper coaching, is to learn how to position yourself on the mound, and how to avoid all those herky-jerky kinds of motions that some young pitchers pick up somewhere along the line.

That is another way that you can hurt your arm. Just remember to deliver the ball every time with your own natural motion. The secret lies in the delivery.

The Delivery

The first thing that you have to do if you want to become a decent pitcher is to develop your own rhythm of throwing, just the same way that you have to develop your own rhythm of batting. And the next thing is to throw all of your pitches with that same basic delivery.

The way that you *can* hurt your arm is if you throw overhand one time and, on the very next pitch, to make it look different, you come around sidearm. Your arm has to be trained in one basic way: The way that is the easiest and the most natural for you. If you are a natural sidearm pitcher, throw that way. If you are a natural overarm pitcher—as most boys are—throw that way. But do it all the time.

It is also a truism that you really can fool the batters if you learn to throw different kinds of pitches out of the same motion. You are more deceptive, because the batter has a more difficult time making up his mind what the pitch is if you use the same basic delivery all the time. In fact, you are accomplishing a dual purpose. You are fooling the batter more, and you're giving your arm more protection.

You hurt your arm when you throw overhand ninety-nine times out of a hundred, and then you get in a jam with a batter whom you figure you absolutely have to get out—maybe the score is tied and the opposing winning run is on third—and you come in with the ball sidearm. There are two reasons you shouldn't do that. First, sidearm obviously isn't your most effective way of pitching or you'd have been using it all along. Second, your muscles just aren't ready for that kind of sudden shift and you can easily pull one.

I think another thing that may contribute to sore arms in the Little League is that too many youngsters have a propensity for thinking too far ahead. Just as far too many Little League hitters want to be able to slug the ball like a Frank Howard, far too many Little League pitchers want to be able to pitch like Bob Gibson.

They worry that their fast ball isn't fast enough or their change-up isn't slow enough, and they start trying to force pitches and, what is worse, force themselves. Little Leaguers ought to just worry about how well they compete against their contemporaries, and not worry about major leaguers—or even youngsters ahead of them in the Babe Ruth League. It may not only make them strain too much, but it may have another result. If they worry about it too much, it may begin to undermine their confidence, to make them doubt their own abilities, and this is a much greater danger.

This is a nice point for adults—parents, coaches, and managers—to keep in mind. You want the boy to play up to his potential, and you know he won't improve and get stronger if he isn't always testing himself to see how much he can do, but you have to guard against his trying too hard, straining too much.

The way major leaguers avoid this is through the Spring

training program. Don Newcombe, for example, used to amaze me. I don't know of any pitcher who worked harder in Spring training than Don Newcombe, because he knew how important it was. He was a big man too, you know, and I think it's generally harder for a big man to get into shape than for an ordinary-sized fellow. He ran more than any man on the squad and then he'd get off on the sidelines and start throwing. He'd throw real easy for the first couple of days, then gradually throw harder and harder, preparing himself, till after a few weeks he was up at full speed. He was a great fast-ball pitcher and I believe two things contributed to that. One was his natural physique, which was big and strong, but the other was that he trained so hard during Spring training that when the season opened, he was ready, he wasn't holding back for fear of straining himself.

He didn't overstrain himself by getting tense and trying to aim the ball instead of pitching it. He kept himself as relaxed as possible, and he had a smooth overhand delivery. He very seldom had a sore arm.

Now, Spring training isn't available to a Little Leaguer, so the problem has to be handled in a different way. First, the coach or the manager should be able to spot a boy who's over-trying, and should talk to him. Try to find out if he is trying to throw harder than he can, tell him he can ruin his effectiveness by doing that. And his parents, too, should be able to reassure him that he's doing as well, or better, than his contemporaries. A boy can fall into the trap of thinking that everything depends on one game, or on one pitch.

Another thing to guard against is the bad habit that youngsters can get into in the Little League, of throwing the wrong way. A young pitcher will often find that throwing with an odd delivery, with maybe a little hitch in it, will get strikes on a batter, and he'll tend to throw that way all the time.

Maybe that way of pitching can get batters out in the Little Leagues, but if you want to go on in baseball, maybe in the Babe Ruth League or in high school, you should practice getting batters out with the smoothest delivery you can get. Never mind trying to find some tricky way of delivering the ball that may end up by hurting your arm.

When I was with the Dodgers we had a pitcher named Jack Banta, who was a sidearm pitcher, which is perfectly okay except that Jack had a kind of jerky motion, not smooth like Newcombe's, and finally his arm gave out on him entirely.

You can practice control all by yourself, as I described in Chapter One. Simply find a backstop someplace and get your two sticks and string, and make your own strike zone. The first thing you should concentrate on is simply getting the ball over the plate. Don't try to aim it, just use your natural throwing motion. After you've gotten to the point that you feel you can get the ball through the rectangle most of the time, then try your hand at even finer control. Never mind trying to shave the corner of the plate, just see if you can move it up and down, and from side to side. If you practice that consistently, by the time you are too old for Little League, you should have a fair amount of control.

Keep Your Eye on the Mitt

Practicing by yourself, you have to imagine there's a catcher's mitt where you're trying to throw it. Imagine the mitt up high or down low, in or out. The reason for trying to develop that sort of control as soon as possible is that, as you know, all hitters have weaknesses and strengths, even the great ones. Some of them will murder a high ball and hit a little blooper on a low one. Some like pitches inside and some outside.

When you're actually pitching, you *have* to keep your eye on the catcher's mitt. Just watch any major league pitcher.

There are some who turn their bodies two-thirds of the way around from the catcher, and there are some who rear so far back you'd swear none of them could see the catcher's mitt, but if you look closely you'll see they really do have their eyes on the mitt. If you do turn too much, as your pitching improves, you will lose sight of the mitt for a fraction of a second and then you'll find that you have to jerk your body or jerk your throw to compensate for it.

But that lies in the future. What you have to concentrate on in Little League is to get that ball over the plate.

The Field Director and Conditioning

This brings me to catching, the position I consider the most difficult to play and, if we put pitching aside, the most vital position on the team.

The catcher simply has to know every aspect of the game. He has to act as a sort of field director for his team, for the very simple reason that he's the only player on the field who can see all the other players all the time.

In addition to that, if you want to continue catching, you'll find you have to know as much about opposing batters as the pitcher, and maybe more. The catcher may notice that a certain hitter is changing his stance a little, and the way to pitch to him today is not the way the pitcher on the mound pitched to him the last time. In addition, the catcher is closer to the pitcher than any other man on the team—I don't mean in a physical sense, I mean in the sense that the catcher can spot first whether the pitcher still has his overpowering stuff, or whether he's tiring a little and his fast ball isn't quite as fast, or maybe his curve isn't breaking as well as it should.

Sometimes you may even see a catcher motioning to a fielder in one way or another. It's because, knowing the game and the hitter and the pitcher as well as he does, and from his position where he can see the entire field, he figures maybe the fielder isn't playing this particular hitter right.

The basics of Little League catching should come from your manager: How to squat, the necessity of holding the mitt top up and with the face toward the pitcher so that you present him with a target, the necessity of keeping your right hand closed into a fist until the ball is in the mitt, so that you don't end up with a broken finger.

And one of the problems you'll face in Little League is the problem of stopping balls from getting by you, just because most young Little League pitchers have a propensity for uncorking a wild one every now and then. But the principle of an infielder smothering a ground ball if he can't catch it, applies here. If you see the pitch is wild, try to knock it down and smother it; if it's too far away, go after it as fast as you can the best way you can.

A catcher has to be strong, and he has to be in terrific shape. It's not just those one-hundred-and-twenty pounders who come barreling in to home plate, trying to stretch a triple into a homer and perfectly willing to knock you into the backstop in the hope that you'll drop the ball; it's also the amount of squatting that you have to do, the number of times that you have to jump up for the throw to second and the weight of the equipment that you have to wear.

I hate to think of the number of deep knee bends that the average major league catcher does every year to get into, and to stay in shape.

But catching has its own rewards, basically in the importance of the job itself. If you want to be a catcher—most of the ones I knew preferred it to any other position—you just have to face up to the fact that you'll have to develop the strongest legs on the team.

Catchers are rare, and good catchers are gems beyond compare. If you are a good catcher, the chances of your making a team, whether it's in the Little League or higher up in organized ball, are much better than a player at any other position.

The Pop-up

It's a pity you don't get more chance at pop-ups in the Little League, since pop-ups are the hardest balls I know to field.

The ball comes in with a spinning motion, the batter swings and pops it a hundred feet in the air. Between the spinning motion of the ball and the slice of the bat, the ball can go almost anywhere. The problem the catcher faces is that, even if the ball is playable, for the first half-second or so, he doesn't know precisely where it is. He has to snap up to his feet, jerk off his mask, pick up the ball against the sky, and get over to it. He has to remember to hold onto his mask until he knows where he's going, and then throw it off to one side. Obviously, if you toss your mask away before you spot the ball, you may find that you've tossed it right in the path that you have to run.

Another problem about pop-ups is that it's hard to practice them. If you're practicing any other kind of fielding, a fungo hitter can hit fly balls to you, or he can hit grounders, but deliberately hitting pop-ups is impossible.

Yet, if you want to be a catcher, it's one of the most important kind of plays you can make.

Occasionally, in Little League, you will have a ball hit so that it clears the cage and goes almost straight up. You should take advantage of your opportunity there. If you're catching, you should make a stab at going after them. You may only get one out of ten, but that still counts as an out.

As a matter of fact, I know of Little League coaches who go to great lengths to teach their catchers how to go after pop flies. They will get the catcher in full gear behind the plate, with a batter standing at the plate in front of him, and then throw the ball up in the air to make it look like a pop

CATCHING
THE POP-UP

CATCHING: THE POP UP/ Jump to your feet, throw off the mask, hold onto mas
until you know where you're going, then toss it to one side.

fly. It isn't the same thing, of course, but it gives the catcher the rough idea of what he has to do.

Some managers don't want their catchers to jerk off the mask before they go after the ball, and I have no quarrel with them. I personally prefer to have young players jerk off the mask, because it is easier to spot where the ball is that way. It also gives young players practice in what they ought to be doing, and what they'll have to learn how to do at some stage if they ever want to be real catchers.

Considering the number of pop flies a Little League catcher is able to get in a season, I think it's better for them to learn this than to keep the mask on and make maybe one more play in the year.

There are all sorts of fine points like this that are up to the individual managers and coaches. Take the matter of bunts or topped balls. The catcher more than any other player is faced with the problem of going after a ball in one direction when he's going to have to throw in another—which is about the most difficult throw. Take a ball that is bunted or topped down the third base line.

Some coaches want their catchers to make a sort of half-circle run to the left of the ball in fielding it, so that when they come up with the ball, they're more or less facing first. In this way he not only is facing first but he keeps the first baseman in his vision without having to make a big turn.

The Throw to Second

The throw to second is another skill that you can practice by yourself—with someone to act as second baseman, of course. I mention the throw to second only—although you obviously will have to be able to throw to first and third—because by all odds it's the most frequent and demanding that the catcher is called upon to make.

There's more to the throw than just getting rid of the ball, accurately, and with snap behind it. You have to get your whole body set. If you watch a big league catcher you see how he jumps to position, his body and his arm in position. A good catcher is always prepared to throw, for his vision can be blocked by the hitter and a delayed steal could result unless he is ready. The catcher knows, too, that the short-stop always will backup the throw to second base automatically.

If you watch a big league catcher make the throw, you'll see that it comes from right beside his right ear, a real snap throw with plenty on it. The reason is that the catcher doesn't have the time to get his arm all the way back to get something on the ball. He has to snap that elbow up, get his hand back beside his ear, and fire that ball down to second.

It's the same old thing about the matter of inches and split seconds. The extra split second that it would take him to get his arm all the way back to make the throw could be the difference between *safe* and *out*. Just figure that that split second would give the runner time to make one more stride, and then figure the number of times you've seen a runner safe at second because he beat the throw by just that margin.

I know that while you're still playing Little League ball you don't have the strength in your arm or shoulder to make the throw the way a grown man with four or five years in organized ball can, but work your way up to it gradually.

At eleven or twelve, you have to bring your arm back a little farther and maybe out a little, to make the throw. What you want to be able to do, as you get stronger, is to bring that arm back approximately to your ear. On each pitch, jump to a throwing position if you possibly can. It's a wonderful way to remind yourself of what you should be doing.

In practicing the throw, you should make a constant adjustment between what you can do, and what you want to do. In other words, your first duty is to get that ball down to the second baseman in order to get an out, and you'll need a little extra time to get your strength behind the throw. What you gradually want to do is to cut down on the time it takes you to make the throw.

In a game, you can't worry about all the fine points of your throwing. In a game, you just fire the ball as best you can. It's in practice where you should develop your throw.

Summary

These are the main points for pitchers and catchers:

THE PITCHER

1. *Develop a smooth, rhythmic delivery.*
2. *Develop your speed gradually.*
3. *Use the same motion for all pitches.*
4. *Keep your eye on the mitt.*

THE CATCHER

1. *Know the whole game.*
2. *Practice snap throws.*
3. *Practice getting pop-ups.*
4. *Always keep the ball in front of you.*

6

●●●●●●●●●●●

THE OUTFIELD

In the major leagues, the main thing that is looked for in an outfielder is the ability to produce runs. In the majors, you automatically assume that an outfielder can catch the ball and that he has the arm to fire it back. But most fielders can do this, so the premium is on hitting ability.

That isn't true in Little League. The Little League manager who has a hitter who can produce runs is indeed a lucky man. But still, there are three qualities that I'd look for in a Little League outfielder. They are: Power, speed, and arm.

The most important thing that the Little League outfielder has to learn—as opposed to what he can do—is concentration. I'd like to discuss that a little, then talk about the roles of:

1. THE CENTER FIELDER
2. THE RIGHT FIELDER
3. THE LEFT FIELDER

Then I'd like to make some general points that apply to all three.

The reason I emphasize concentration so much is that it can make you a much better player.

Joe DiMaggio used to specialize in making what seemed like impossible catches look like the easiest thing in the world. Part of it, I'm sure—apart from his great reflexes and experience—was due to his concentration. It seemed to me he concentated so hard on what was going on at the plate that, at the crack of the bat, he would know whether the pitch had been inside or outside, and he would start for the ball at that very same instant.

He also had an uncanny ability that I often marvelled at: knowing how far the ball had been hit—whether it was a long ball that he'd have to go back for, or whether he'd have to start charging in for it.

Judging how far the ball is hit isn't easy at first. It's something that comes with experience, but again it's helped by complete concentration on what's going on at the plate when the pitcher is throwing the ball to the batter.

The Center Fielder

The center fielder is the key to the outfield. He should be one of the best and most experienced players on the team. You've often heard that every good ball club has to have "strength up the middle." That means a good catcher, good shortstop and second baseman, and a good center fielder.

The center fielder should have the best reflexes and the best speed, because it's part of his job to back up the two other outfielders, as well as backing up second base when there's a throw made there. He should have the best arm of the outfielders.

The center fielder should also be in charge of outfield plays, calling out the name of the fielder to take the ball so that you don't have two youngsters colliding while trying to make the same catch, with the ball falling in between them.

The Right Fielder

I think that the right fielder should be the next best and most experienced player in the outfield, because in my experience with Little League, most batted balls that get out of the infield go into right. This is due to the fact that most

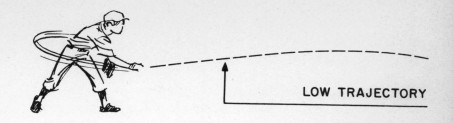

LOW TRAJECTORY

OUTFIELD

HEELS OFF GROUND

OUTFIELD: SOME BASIC MOVES/For grounders, charge the ball and come up throwing, keeping your throw on as low a trajectory as possible. For flies, run on the balls of your feet, keeping heels off the ground.

hitters of this age—I'm thinking now of right-handed hitters —have a tendency to swing behind the ball and so to push it.

The right fielder also should have a throwing arm second only to the center fielder's, because he's likely to have more throws—and longer throws—to make than the left fielder.

The Left Fielder

Here is a good place for the youngest or least experienced outfielder on the team. He doesn't have to cover the amount of ground that the center fielder does, and he's not likely to have the number of plays that the right fielder will have. In fact, considering the relatively few fly balls that are hit to left field in the Little League, most of the young left fielders' duties will consist of coming in for ground balls and getting them back into the infield.

Now as to my general points: To get experience in judging fly balls, I think that when you're in practice, your fungo hitter should hit them to your right and to your left, out over your head or in front of you, without letting you know in advance where the ball is going.

You'll find that pretty soon you can judge the balls off on either side of you pretty well. Then, as you get more practice and experience, you'll begin to get the knack of judging whether you have to come in for the ball or go back for it.

Considering the size of most Little League fields, I think that you should play back rather than in—for the very simple reason that it's easier to come in for a ball than it is to go back for it.

As to your exact position in the outfield—back more or in more, more to your right or left—should be left to your manager, who will know more about the opposing hitters than you do. You should be alert to signals from the manager or coach as to where you should be playing.

The reason that positioning in the outfield is important—

and will become more important the longer you play—is the necessity of denying the extra base to the runner.

Especially if the score is close, you've got to be positioned as correctly as you can in the outfield to get the ball as quickly as you can. And you've got to make sure that the ball doesn't get by you.

If it's a home run over the fence, that's one thing, but if it's a ground ball, charge it! Like an infielder, don't let the ball play you, you play it. Watch any top outfielder, watch the way he charges the ball. He knows the only way he's going to be able to throw out a base runner if the ball is hit through the infield is to be charging in, moving toward the infield, coming up throwing. Throwing that way, too, lets you get a little bit extra on the ball.

I think it's a great help for an outfielder to work out as much as he can in the infield so that he gets as much experience as he can in fielding ground balls. You'll find it invaluable practice for the outfield.

You have another thing to watch out for in Little League. You have to charge in to get the ball, but—as I said—you've got to make sure that it doesn't get by you. Major league outfields are kept in pretty top shape by the groundskeepers. Little League outfields are apt to have bumps in them. If a ground ball is hit to you in the outfield and you can't play the way you want to, at least block it. It's bad enough for an infielder to let the ball get by him, but he has an outfielder backing him up. If an outfielder lets it through, it can be fatal.

Once you have the ball, get it back to the infield just as fast as you can. Never hold the ball in the outfield. As a matter of fact, I'd get into the habit of getting the ball back in as fast as I could whether there are runners on base or not.

If you get into the habit of holding it when there are no runners on base, sooner or later the day will come when there is one man out and a man on first, and you hold the ball just long enough to let him get to third instead of holding him at second. On the next play there's a long fly ball and a run scores. If you'd held the runner at second, he never could have scored on a fly.

In addition, don't start running in with it, which can develop into another bad habit. Throw it. You know you can throw a ball a lot faster than you can run with it. Even if your throw is a little off-line and maybe isn't quite far enough, the infielder can take over from there.

Lord knows the number of times, even in the major leagues, I've seen a runner get an extra base just because an outfielder took four or five extra steps getting ready to make his throw, giving a really heads-up runner just that tiny extra fraction of time he needed to go on.

The outfield throw is another one that you have to practice to make better the longer you play. If you make a high sweeping throw, it takes longer to get in than one that's on a lower trajectory, and again it may give a runner a chance to go on. It should be as close on line as you can make it, because very often a throw that is dead on the line will make a runner hold up, but the main thing is to get it in fast and on as low a trajectory as you can.

Circumstances always determine where you throw, which is why I keep stressing concentration so much, knowing exactly what's going on in the game at all times.

In a close ball game, the score generally determines where you throw. Basically, you go after the tying run. If the runner going home is the tying run, go after him. If the batter is the tying run, try to keep him down to a single.

To give another illustration: Say it's late in the game, the score is 2-0 in favor of your team, there's a runner on second, the ball is hit to you on the ground. Don't try for the runner going home; just make sure you hold the batter at first, where he will need at least a double to score. If you let him get to second he will be able to score on a single and the game will be all tied up. If you hold him at first, the farthest he should be able to go on a single is to third.

Let me give you another example about how circumstances determine where you throw. Say a man is on first and the batter hits the ball to you playing in right field. Your throw should be to the cut-off man, the shortstop, who should have stationed himself between second and third.

Your throw should be hard and flat as you can make it and still be sure that it will get to the cut-off man. The best thing to do is to aim at his head. That way you won't get the ball too high, and he'll be able to see it better.

If your throw is too high and arching, the runner can easily move up a base, and putting a runner in a scoring position in a tight game is not the sign of a thinking ball player.

I'll give you the most dramatic instance I know of where outfield play changed the course of a game—indeed, of a whole series. Unfortunately, as far as I'm concerned, it's the play that cost the Brooklyn Dodgers any chance at the 1950 pennant, and it was due to our coach at third, who wasn't watching what was happening on the field or he wasn't thinking. It all adds up to the same thing.

It was the last day of the season, the last game, and the Philadelphia Phillies held a one-game lead over us. We just had to win this game to get into the play-offs.

It was the last inning, the score was tied, and we were at bat. Since the game was being played in Brooklyn, all we needed was one run to win the game.

We had men on first and second and nobody out. Duke Snider came up to bat. Duke was a real strong hitter. Cal Abrams, our man on second, was edging off the bag.

I didn't see what happened, from where I was, but from what newspapermen later wrote, Granny Hamner, the Phillies' shortstop, flashed a pick-off sign to Stan Lopata, the Phillies' catcher. There was strategy behind the move. Snider was a left-handed batter, so Hamner, cheating a little —as I mentioned about how you make the double play—

was playing over closer to second than he normally would have been. For the pick-off, Hamner would get in behind Abrams and take the throw. I don't think they really expected to pick-off Abrams, they just wanted to keep him close so that if Snider got a hit, they'd have a chance to nail Abrams at the plate.

Anyway, out in center field, Richie Ashburn of the Phillies got the sign and he began to edge in toward second so that he could come in to back up the throw, in case it got by Hamner. Now, it's no discredit to our third base coach that he didn't notice these subtle moves—but no one else did either. Then came the play.

The pitch that the Phillies' pitcher, Robin Roberts, threw, I have no explanation for. Maybe he misunderstood Lopata's signal for the pitchout, maybe the ball got away from him. At any rate, the pitch came straight in over the plate and Snider rapped it out to center. But the instant Roberts had let go of the ball, Ashburn had started charging in for his back-up play, so that when Snider's ball hit, Ashburn had it on one hop about forty feet on the grass behind second, and he fired home.

If our third base coach had noticed Ashburn charging in, it might not have been a disaster, but he didn't notice until it was too late. Instead of holding Abrams up at third, he'd waved him on. Ashburn's throw had him out by a mile.

If the coach had been able to hold Abrams up, we would have had men on first, second and third, and nobody out. As it was, we had men on second and third and one out. I was walked intentionally to set up a double-play possibility, but Carl Furillo popped up, the next man hit an easy fly, and we were out of the inning. In the top half of the next inning, Dick Sisler hit a home run for the Phillies into the left field stands. We didn't score in the bottom half of the inning and so we were out of the game, and out of the play-offs.

I've told this anecdote to illustrate that we might have had a chance at the Series except for the fact that one man, and an experienced baseball man at that, thought he knew what was going to happen, and let his concentration waver just that little bit.

In baseball, you just can't do it.

If you don't get into the habit of concentrating that way —and you should make it a habit—what happened to us that day with the Phillies can happen to your team.

In addition, when you're in the outfield, concentrating on every pitch means that you'll be able to figure whether the pitch was inside or outside, and so you'll be able to judge whether it's heading directly to you, whether it's off to the right or the left. The minute you pick up the flight of the ball, you have to start moving toward where it's going to be when it comes down. You can't wait till it's half-way out to you.

You've heard of great outfielders like Mays and Di-Maggio, and the way people say they seemed to start running for the place where the ball would come down the minute they heard the crack of the bat. That's not precisely true. The real point is that they knew the opposing hitters so well, they concentrated hard on every pitch. Just the way the batter swung gave them a clue as to the general area where the ball was going and they started out instantly, looking for the exact flight of the ball. It takes years of experience to be able to do something like that—plus the reflexes that a Mays or a DiMaggio has. A Little Leaguer should simply concentrate on picking up the flight of the ball. Judging fly balls is strictly a matter of experience, but you'll never learn if you're not getting yourself set as the pitcher is getting set, and following the flight of the ball in to the batter.

There's one final point I'd like to make about outfield play, and that's how you run when you're fielding a fly ball. Run on the balls of your feet, just the way track athletes do. Keep your heels off the ground.

The reason that runners on track teams do it is because it gives them greater speed. Playing the outfield, you have an additional reason for it. If you're running for a fly ball and let your heels hit the ground, you get a kind of jolting action through your body, and that throws your eyes off focus. Every time your heel hits the ground, the ball seems to jump a little.

I remember when I first played the outfield—I was shifted out there for a while—we were playing in Philadelphia. The ball was hit in the air maybe a hundred feet past the infield and I came charging in for it. Just as I was about to reach it I came down on my heels and suddenly the ball seemed to bobble on me.

I stuck out my glove thinking it was down but it was up and it almost hit me on the top of my head, which is pretty embarassing for a major league outfielder. A lot of times you'll see an outfielder running for a ball and you're sure he's going to catch it, but suddenly it bounces off his shoulder or his glove and you say, ah, he should have had it, how could he miss a ball like that?

I always think it's because he suddenly came down on his heels.

Summary

These are the important points for outfielders:

1. *Concentrate*
2. *Play position on the batter.*
3. *Charge grounders; block them if necessary.*
4. *Get the ball back in, fast.*
5. *Throw as flat as you can.*
6. *Run on the balls of your feet.*

7

TEAMWORK AND SPORTSMANSHIP

There's a lot more to Little League baseball than how well you hit a ball, or throw it, or catch it. Two of the other elements—teamwork and sportsmanship—are, in my opinion, more important in the long run than the techniques of baseball because they will be of value to you all through your life.

To me, these two elements have one thing in common—respect for the other fellow. Teamwork to me means getting along with your fellow players, working with them—whether you like them or not. I've known pitchers, for example, who were heartily disliked by one or more of the other players on the team, and maybe deep in their secret hearts they would have liked to see him get shelled. But it never showed while they were playing with him. The good of the team was more important than their own personal feelings. They'd work just as hard to make a double play for him as they would for a pitcher who was really popular.

The same way with sportsmanship—it means treating other players, whether they're on your team or not, as fellows humans, whether you like them personally or not.

The essence of teamwork is the willingness of the individual players to sacrifice themselves for the good of the team. A winning baseball team, just like a winning football team must have a group of players working as one; each trying to help the other, each doing his absolute best to insure the success of the whole group instead of each player thinking of his own personal glory.

Very often in an important series, after a game, the reporters would come to me and say, well, how did you feel when you got that triple, or how did you feel when you made that catch.

Invariably, my answer was, let's wait till we've won the pennant, or won the World Series, before we start talking about one play in one game, because if the team as a whole loses the pennant or the Series, what one man did on one play makes very little difference.

If you have a winning team, all the good plays made during the season by each player—even the ones who didn't hit the home runs or make the spectacular catches, but helped the team nonetheless—all add up to the reason that your team won. If the team loses, the outstanding plays made by individuals don't really add up to very much.

I remember, very well, my junior college days when I was playing football for Pasadena Junior College in California. I was the quarterback for the team, and there's nothing like being a quarterback to teach you the value of teamwork. In those days, the quarterback called all the signals without any help from the sidelines, and I was very well aware of the dependence I had on the linemen up front and on the blocking backs, and I used to try to figure out what was important to them.

For instance, when we got into scoring position, I didn't care who scored as long as we got on the board, so I'd call on the fullback or one of the blocking backs to take it in. If they didn't score, they'd come back to the huddle and tell me to call my own play, knowing that with an added blocker I'd have a pretty good chance of getting the ball in, which was partly the reason I was such a high scorer.

I remember once way back in junior high school our team got to arguing about who should get more credit for winning games, the line or the backfield. I admit it was a silly argument to get into, but there it was. The backs said they were the ones making the touchdowns, the linemen said they were the ones opening the holes and if it weren't for them the backs would never be able to get anywhere. Very frankly, it wasn't too long before we weren't playing together as a team.

Then came the final game of a season in which we hadn't been defeated. We weren't too far into the game before we found ourselves behind. It looked as though we would get further behind, too, so we called a time out. Someone said: "Look, we're going to lose this game if we don't start playing together the way we used to and stop arguing about who's doing the most to win; we're not playing against the other team, we're playing against each other."

To make a long story short, we began to buckle down and finally we pulled the game out.

I have one final anecdote about Pasadena Junior College that I include simply because I believe it shows how the teamwork that is necessary in athletics can overcome even something as ugly as racial prejudice.

In my first year, in 1937, we had a new coach who had come out from Oklahoma and he had brought with him six very fine football players, all of whom were white and who had never had any previous experience playing with blacks. Fortunately, they turned out to be pretty sensible guys who were more interested in playing football than in the color of your skin.

One thing that did happen which was no fault of theirs illustrates that racial discrimination can work if you want it to work. We had three of the best ends in Southern California, all black, and all of them left ends. There's no doubt in my mind that one of them would have been the regular right end, but the "quota" system for black players was working, and a white end had that position. The black players were not even given a chance to try out. That's the way it can be done if you want to hold down on the number of black players you have on your team; have two or three of them at the same position, so that it leaves other positions open for whites. When you substitute at that one position, you substitute another black.

These tactics were part of the system then and are still practiced at some colleges now. However, in our case, the result of the blacks and whites playing together on our team led, I think, to a tremendous growth of understanding on both sides.

When we were finished with our playing season, one of the white fellows came up to me and said, you know, we have such a great team spirit and we work together so well, why don't we all go to the same college together?

I think one of the tragedies of this nation is that people don't get a chance to know each other. They don't get a chance, as these white fellows from the South did, of playing with blacks. They don't get a chance to learn what motivates individuals, makes us do the kinds of things we do.

That Pasadena Junior College team won sixteen consecutive ball games, after a bad start, and I'm sure it was because we learned team spirit and an understanding of one another. When we got on the ball field, regardless of what section of the country the players came from or what the color of their skin was, we played for Pasadena Junior College and we knew that the only way we could win was if we played as one.

One of the compliments that I still treasure most came from Wilbur Johns, my basketball coach at the University of California at Los Angeles. Johns said that he thought I was perhaps the most unselfish basketball player he had ever coached. What brought that about was an incident that showed I was willing to sacrifice my own personal advantage for the good of the team.

He cited one particular game where we were leading by a point or two late in the game. It was also late in the season, and I was in a battle for the scoring title with Ralph Vaughan of the University of Southern California. I had a fairly easy driving lay-up shot that I figured on making most of the time, and I got the ball and started in. Then I pulled up and started dribbling back out because I knew that I only had to stall for a minute or so, and we'd win the game by not taking any shots.

Wilbur Johns felt that a different type of player, who would have been more concerned about winning the scoring title than in his team's victory, and would have gone for the goal even though it would have meant giving the ball up to the other team.

But I believe in sacrificing, for I believe that you come out better in the long run by thinking more of your team than of yourself. I've tried to live by that philosophy, and even though it's gotten me into discouraging spots at times, I still believe in it.

I remember one particular game against the New York Giants back in the days when the Giants-Dodger's games would fill the ball park every time. Sal Maglie was the Giants' pitcher in that game. Sal was called "The Barber," and he was not called that for nothing. He was a master at dusting a batter off, he was very good at keeping you off balance, and he had no hesitation at all in throwing so close that you had to jump back to get out of the way of the ball.

In this game, he was dusting us off pretty regularly.

So, at one point in the game, in the dugout, our team captain, Peewee Reese, looked down the bench and said:

"Okay, we've got to do something about Maglie—*Jack.*"

You notice who the "we" came down to. But Reese had a reason for it: I was one of the best on the team at laying down a bunt where I wanted to.

We talked it over on the bench and we decided that when I got up to bat, I was to push a bunt down the first base line and when Maglie came in to field it, I was to try to take him all the way out to right field to show him that he couldn't use the brush-back technique against the Dodgers. Or, if he did, we knew ways to retaliate.

When I got up to the batting circle, our bat boy, who had listened to the entire conversation on the bench, was waiting for me. The bat boy was a very nice guy. Most people thought he was a young kid, he was so small, but actually he was as old as most of the players on the team. He also, unfortunately, had a very bad heart condition of which he died a few years later, still in his twenties. At the batting circle, he said to me:

"Jack, why don't you let one of the other guys do it? It always seems to me that when there's something to do for the good of the team, you're always the guy that has to do it."

I don't know what kind of mood I was in, but I remember looking at him and thinking, yeah, let someone else do it, why does it always have to be me? And I told him:

"You're right. Let somebody else do it."

But when I got up to the plate I could hear Reese calling: "Okay, Jack, let's go," and I changed my mind. I decided that Maglie shouldn't be allowed to get away with what he was doing, and I knew there weren't too many other guys on the team as good as I was at bunting. The play sort of worked.

I say "sort of" because when I did lay down the bunt toward first, wise old Maglie didn't take a step away from the mound. Instead, the first baseman fielded the ball and the young second baseman, a small fellow named Davey Williams, covered first and took the throw.

Here is where the unfortunate part of that play happened. Davey, as I say, was a good deal smaller than I was and he'd had no part whatever of the business of Sal Maglie dusting us back. He shouldn't have to pay for Maglie's sins.

But there was absolutely no way in which I could have

avoided running into him, because in covering first he didn't get off the base line, as he undoubtedly would have if he'd had more time; but the play had developed so fast that by this time I was practically on first base and I ran right into him.

I was really sorry about that development because a perfectly innocent guy was hit, but that sort of thing can happen in the majors. I certainly wouldn't want to see something like that in the Little League, though it does have a good object lesson for Little Leaguers: The base line belongs to the base runner.

I might add that a couple of innings later there was a sequel to the Davey Williams play. It involved Alvin Dark, the Giants' captain and a player whom I admired very much, partly because he thought a lot like I did, and he played on the same general principles that I did.

This incident also illustrates how one thing leads to another in major league ball. It would never happen in the Little League because in Little League you don't have pitchers like Sal Maglie, capable of dusting off a batter again and again without actually hitting him. Dusting off in the Little League is strictly a matter of accident.

Dark, however, thought I had run into Davey out of malice. He got pretty sore, and when he hit the ball to left field the next time he got up at plate, instead of stopping at first as he normally did, he kept on going.

He would have been out by twenty feet and he knew it, but I realized what he had in mind. Most of all he wanted a crack at me. There was only one flaw in his plan. I think that anybody who has ever played baseball or football knows that the runner who is charging down on you, once he commits himself, can't change direction at top speed, so all that I had to do was to fake one way and, when he committed himself, to step back out of his way.

I tried to tag Dark as hard as I could but the tag sort of rolled off his shoulder. Knowing what Dark had in mind I was prepared. Fortunately for Al, I wasn't able to protect myself as I intended.

Anyhow, the entire episode finally ended on that development. And it all started because I was trying to make a play for the good of the team. Within the rules of the game, you must be willing to take as much as you give.

I remember one game I played in the major leagues, the first and only time that I ever was fined—and deservedly so —was when I decided to disobey orders and hit away rather than bunt.

We had men on first and second, nobody out. It was an obvious bunt situation and my manager, Burt Shotten, gave the bunt sign. I stepped up to the plate and as I recall it the first pitch was way off and I didn't even offer at it. I saw the third baseman was playing in so far that I felt if he took one more step he'd practically be standing on my shoes. I was thinking to myself, boy, all I've got to do is hit the ball a little past the third baseman and I've got myself a base hit.

I was pretty good at pulling the ball and I made up my mind, all on my own and against Burt Shotten's orders, that I'd swing away. I did. I hit a little chopper right straight to the third baseman. He got it on the first hop and threw to second, the second baseman got it and threw to first. It was a double play.

If I had bunted successfully, I would have moved the runners to second and third, with one out, putting two men in scoring position. The result of the game is not important.

The point is that I disobeyed the manager, and I was fined for it, as I should have been. As a matter of fact, even if I'd gotten a hit and a run had scored, I still should have been fined, and I would have been. I know the way Shotten thought—if you disobeyed him, you were fined, run or no run.

Later in my career, I disagreed with a lot of things a manager told me to do, and sometimes I was right and sometimes I was wrong. But I made it a rule, after the bunt incident, to follow the manager's orders, no matter what. If a manager told me to do something, I did it, regardless of how I felt.

In the game where I was fined, I tried to manage as well as play. It's important to allow the manager to make the decision.

I might point out that there is also a very practical side to teamwork on a baseball team.

For example, if you're a pitcher trying to keep book on all the batters in the League, you'd have a full time job on your hands. But with everyone on your team, from the manager and the coaches down to the youngest player, all watching how opposing batters hit, which pitches they're likely to murder and which ones they hit straight to an infielder, you're that much further ahead of the game.

The same way with a batter. Other batters can help you on what pitch the pitcher is most likely to come through with in a given situation.

This sort of working together can be especially useful in base stealing. If you had to rely only on your own observation to try to figure out whether a pitcher was going to throw to the batter, or whether he was going to try a pick-off, it might be half a season before you are able to pick up his moves. As I said in my section on base running, pitchers spend months and years on perfecting their pick-off moves. In addition, first base isn't the best place to study a pitcher's motion.

But if you have a whole teamful of guys studying the pitcher's moves, if there's a tip-off, sooner or later one of them will spot it.

The essence of teamwork, you see, includes two factors: Your willingness to sacrifice yourself for the good of your team, plus the ability of all the players on the team to work together for the good of all.

Good sportsmanship, especially in relationship to your fellow players, is part of teamwork.

For example, if your team has lost because one of your outfielders dropped a sure fly ball, or because one of your best hitters struck out with the bases loaded, it's all too easy to give way to your natural feelings and jump on the unfortunate player and tell him he ought to go back down to the cap league. It's the easy way to get rid of your own frustrations and anger at having lost the game.

But think of it this way—that player probably already feels bad enough. And I don't think it's the place of one player to criticize another.

I still remember a game in Milwaukee when Jim Gilliam, our second baseman, didn't slide in what turned out to be a crucial play, and it cost us the ball game. Most of us felt pretty bad about it, but we felt it was the manager's place to make any criticism. However, our catcher, Roy Campanella, did criticize Gilliam. In the very next game, the very same thing happened—except that this time it was Campanella who didn't slide. When we asked Gilliam afterwards why he didn't get on Campy, he just said that he didn't think it was his place. It was the manager's.

That's the sort of attitude you should have toward your fellow players.

As far as your own personal display of feelings is concerned—for example, suppose you're called out on strikes in a tight situation—I think it's only human to let off steam, within the limits that the rules allow.

You know that you can't argue with an umpire over called strikes, and you know that bat-throwing will get you thrown out of the game. For a very good reason, too. Slinging a bat when you're mad can end up with someone getting hurt.

I remember an incident in Milwaukee toward the end of my playing career that I still think of with embarrassment. I went up to bat in a kind of a bad mood because it was drizzling slightly—meaning that the game might soon be called —and Milwaukee had just scored four runs and I didn't see any way we were going to get them back. Then I was called out on strikes and I actually pretended to be madder than I was. I slung my bat, meaning just to sort of get it back toward the dugout, but it skidded and went up into the stands and hit a lady spectator.

I was not only thrown out of the game, as I should have been, but for a time I was threatened with a lawsuit.

So the rule is: *No bat slinging,* though I do appreciate the feelings of a player in a tight situation who's just been called out on strikes and who slams down his bat or throws down his batting helmet. It's only natural, but that's as far as it should go.

Apart from the rules on the sort of unsportsmanlike kind of conduct that can get you thrown out of a game, I think that by the time you get to Little League you should have a fairly good idea of what sportsmanship means. Basically it means applying yourself to the standards of what you expect from others. You expect a certain amount of riding from opposing players, but you know when you feel that they're getting over the line.

It's the same thing as far as your own conduct goes. You know yourself when you're giving another player the sort of riding that's just part of the game. And you know when you go over that line you're in the wrong.

There are some managers who require their teams to give a cheer for the opposing team at the end of every game, no matter who won or lost. I've heard some of the cheers that the losers have given the winners, especially after losing an important game, and I must say that I sympathize with the players. It's awfully hard to get your heart into a cheer for a team that's just beaten you.

I don't have any strong feelings at all about this custom. I leave it strictly up to the way the local league feels. I do think, however, that if you cheer a team after you've beaten them, then you're duty bound to cheer when they beat you. It's part of sportsmanship.

Besides, by the time you're playing Little League ball, you've come far enough in athletics to know that losing is as much a part of the game as winning. You're an athlete, even if a young one, and you have to get so that you can take losing pretty much in your stride. No one ever gets to like it, but you can learn to accept it.

Finally, I think that if you can develop the qualities that both teamwork and sportsmanship demand, you'll find that you're all the better for it yourself. If you make the sacrifice bunt or the hit to right, people won't be cheering the way they would if you had hit the ball out of the park, but you'll know that you did your job. If you tell the outfielder who dropped the ball that could have been the final out: "Tough luck, Johnny," instead of blaming him, you'll find that you feel better yourself.

8

●●●●●●●●●●●●●

THE ADULT ROLE

The part that adults play in the functioning of the Little League is of paramount importance, and their attitude can sometimes make the difference between winning and losing ball. Their role breaks down into two categories:

1. PARENTS
2. COACHES, MANAGERS, UMPIRES, AND OTHERS

Parents

The role of the parents further breaks down into their attitudes toward the game on the field and in the home.

Most parents, obviously, have an enormous influence on their children in both places, and I believe most of the influence is for the good. If I had to make a general criticism it would be that too many parents are too anxious to have their sons star players. My own criterion is that if a boy is playing as well as he can, up to his full potential, there is absolutely nothing more that you can ask of him.

Of course he will have his ups and downs. Trying his hardest, he will make fielding errors, and trying his hardest, he will strike out.

Parents who demand near-perfection from their sons not only forget all the other youngsters on the team—after all, baseball *is* a team game—they also do an injustice to the boy himself.

113

In other segments of life they don't do this. They don't criticize an eleven- or twelve-year-old boy because he isn't a sophomore in college. Yet I've seen fathers, and mothers, yell at a boy for not making a play that I'm not sure a college sophomore could have made. And sometimes, in their zealousness, their criticism isn't directed only at their own children.

I remember my wife once went to a Little League game in Stamford, Connecticut, where our son was playing, a game that I couldn't attend. My wife was held up in traffic and arrived at the game a little late. As she sat down in the stands the woman next to her said:

"Your son just struck out."

My wife tried to play it easy and replied:

"Well, it's not the first time, and it probably won't be the last."

The woman was not satisfied and retorted:

"Yes, but my son was on second and he could have scored!"

It didn't make any difference to her that my son obviously hadn't struck out on purpose. The woman wasn't interested in the game or the team—just that her son was on base and that he might possibly—not guaranteed—have scored. Now, a parent that self-centered, or son-centered, whether it be a mother or father, is not going to have a good influence on the boy.

At first his own common sense is going to tell him that just a break of the game went against him, but if he keeps hearing that sort of thing long enough, he's going to begin to wonder if maybe a teammate *didn't* let him down.

Speaking of my son, as most of you probably know, he eventually had to go to an institution because of a drug problem that I think had at least part of its beginnings in the pressures that were put on him by adults, starting as low as the Little League. I think that most people who really start using drugs are simply trying to get out from under pressures that are too strong for them.

This, at any rate, was true of Jackie. He had pressures put on him that I doubt any twelve-year-old could handle—though, of course, the drug problem came later when still other pressures were added.

The trouble was that even when he was a youngster playing ball, people were always saying, "Oh, you're Jackie Robinson's son," and then they'd go on and talk about some game they'd seen me play in where I'd hit a home run or made a sensational catch or something, with the clear implication of, why wasn't he that good?

That sort of thing just simply shouldn't be done, and especially not with a youngster. Every top ball player is just plain born with the body, with the physical equipment, that's far superior to the average man's. Criticizing someone for not having a body like that is like criticizing him for having brown eyes.

There isn't much that you can do basically to the body that you're born with. You can train yourself and exercise, of course, to achieve your physical peak, but you can't add two inches to your height or build a new set of reflexes. You can ruin your body, if you drink too much or smoke or use drugs, but there's no way you can develop the body to become a top professional ball player unless you're born with it. Take Ted Williams' eyes for example. They said that he could read the label on a phonograph record turning at thirty-three-and-a-third revolutions. To be the superb hitter he was, he had to be born with the reflexes and the rest of his abilities, but a pair of eyes like his comes along once in maybe fifty million.

The fact that my son hadn't been born with the equipment to become a superstar didn't worry me a great deal; I didn't spend any time worrying about it. There are a lot of good and useful things you can do in this life without becoming a top athlete.

But other people, perfect strangers—including parents at Little League games—sort of blamed my son for not measuring up to my capabilities.

I think making these kinds of comparisons is absolutely wrong, no matter whose son is involved. I think it's wrong for parents to compare their son's performance with another player's, no matter what names are involved. I believe in judging players according to how they perform in accordance with their capabilities. I believe in treating them equally, and I don't just mean according to the color of their skin. Actually, I think that racial prejudice has been pretty well licked in baseball as well as in other sports, on the playing field. By the time youngsters grow up it will be licked by the front-office managers, and perhaps in most other areas.

The thing that I resented in some parents, as far as their treatment of my son went, was that they wouldn't take him on his own terms.

Actually, he *was* a good ball player, he didn't disgrace himself on any of the teams he played for, and if the spectators had accepted him as another ball player, I don't think he would have had the problems that he later did. But just because he was Jack Robinson, Junior, he was supposed to get the hits that no one else could get, he was supposed to make the plays that no one else could make.

(As an aside to parents, I'll say that when young Jackie did get into trouble, the most important thing that my wife and I did was to stick by him. I've heard of parents who take the attitude that, well, he got into it himself, let him get out, let him fend for himself. That's absolutely wrong. If a youngster gets into trouble and his parents—the people he relies on the most, whether he admits it or not—if his parents let him down, then he's in even deeper trouble. In our family, my wife and I sat down with young Jackie, and talked with him and did everything we could for him, provided him with treatment, and finally he pulled out of it.

We helped with love and understanding—all parents must.)

I think it's a bad mistake for parents to put too much emphasis on individual achievement rather than on team achievement. Too many parents are inclined to reward a youngster because he got a base hit and then to withhold the reward if he didn't. I think that if you reward a youngster with a soda pop after a game in which he got a hit, you should reward him after every game, win, lose, or draw. As long as he gave his best, attitude and determination should be the criteria.

Playing Little League ball isn't a matter of reward and punishment, and it never should become one. Maybe it is in the major leagues, where your contract for next year depends on what you do this year, but let your son sign his first professional contract before reward and punishment enters into his thinking.

There's another side to this. Withholding rewards—or giving them, based on performance—gives a boy the idea that the only thing that matters is winning. I know that winning has become part of the American way of life, but I don't believe that ten- to twelve-year-old boys should be pressured to the point where they think that winning is the only thing that matters. And if you think that just one soda pop doesn't make that much difference, you don't know how much little things mean to youngsters.

Far from being over-concerned with winning, I think that parents should get more pleasure from seeing a Little League team that can bounce back from defeat, benefit from its mistakes, and go on to win the next game.

Actually, I think the kids understand this better than some parents. (I think that the majority of parents understand it, too; I'm talking to the ones who don't, and somehow they always seem to stick out more.) Most of the kids who go through Little League do it because they like to play ball, they like to be with their friends—and both of these things are more important to them than winning or losing, which is as it should be. There's too little fun in life as it is.

How often have you seen the kids on a Little League team, whether they've won or lost, gathered around the refreshment stand, horsing around and joking? If they lost, sure they didn't like it, but to them baseball is still basically a game they like to play with their friends, and I think it ought to be kept that way. Kids today have enough pressure on them without being pressured to play a professional type of baseball while they're still twelve years old.

I think we're all born with certain capabilities; none of us has equal capabilities in all things. I really feel that making a big thing out of the fact that a youngster has gone five games without getting a hit is the same as if an adult were constantly criticized because he wasn't the president of a bank or a college professor. And a youngster is much more susceptible to pressures because of the simple fact that he is a youngster. An adult is more sure of himself, he's learned to live with pressures.

The role of the parents in the home is, I think, the most important one. A child looks on his home as a refuge, where he is free of the pressures of the outside world. If he's had a good day on the field, it's a place to go back to and brag about how well he did. If he had a bad day, it's a place to go back to and get a little sympathy.

Now, the worst thing that can happen to him is to have a home where his parents don't join in his triumphs, or get a little solace if he's had a tough time.

I think the best thing for parents to do, whether he won or lost, is to ask him how the game went. If he won, it indicates an interest to listen to what catch he made or what ball he hit. If he lost, it gives him a chance to talk out his disappointment.

Children are a lot more realistic than parents sometimes think. If the coach didn't play the boy that day, it's no use telling him that the coach was wrong, that maybe the coach "had it in for him." That's false sympathy, and the boy will probably realize it. Most of the good coaches in Little League don't take a regular player out of the lineup except for an overweening reason, and they generally explain that reason to the boy off to one side, in private.

In addition, criticizing the coach in front of the youngster at home is as bad, I think, as withholding a soda pop if he makes a mistake on the field. It gives him the impression that adults—his parents—think that the coach doesn't make his decisions solely on the basis of what is good for the team. Even in the Little League, a coach who makes his decisions on any other basis isn't going to last too long, and I don't think that any more than a tiny minority ever make decisions on any other basis.

As spectators at a game, I think that first of all parents should recognize that the youngsters, consciously or unconsciously, look up to them as models. Again, I think that eighty or ninety percent of parents conduct themselves as reasonable human beings, but again it's the others who are the most conspicuous.

There are two particular kinds of actions that I don't think parents should indulge in. One is the father who shouts to his son, when he's pitching: "Dust him back!" There are two things against that. First, even a major leaguer has to have top-notch control to be able to dust off a batter without endangering him, and Little League pitchers have enough control problems as it is. Second, it's just plain bush league bad sportsmanship.

The other bad action is really getting on an umpire for a decision. Oh, kidding him if you know him is one thing, but seriously heckling is something that should be just plain out.

What parents should do is to applaud players equally on both teams for a good play, and they should never yell at a youngster for missing a play—or even give a good loud groan.

A major leaguer can shrug it off when the fans get on him for a bad play, but one of the great things a youngster gets out of being in the Little League is a sense of identification with his team, a sense of achievement, and yelling at him—or groaning—can destroy both of these feelings. It can give him the feeling both that he's let his team down, and that he's not as good a ball player as he thinks he is.

Either way, it doesn't contribute to playing winning Little League ball.

We all need this feeling, of belonging. Adults—lawyers, doctors, whatever—rely on a sense of identification, self-identification, if you will, a sense of achievement to make their lives satisfactory.

I know a number of men who played either Little League ball or its equivalent when they were youngsters. Many of them have told me they think that part of their success in life was due to the sense of courage and confidence they got as youngsters on a baseball diamond.

We've all heard of the famous line of the Duke of Wellington that the Battle of Waterloo was won on the playing fields of Eton, and I'm absolutely convinced of the truth of that. You don't suddenly teach the values of courage and confidence to a man, you have to start when he's a youngster.

Coaches, Managers, Umpires, and Others

If there's one group of adults in America for whom I have great admiration, it's those men and women who give up so much of their time to help the Little League—including the mothers who man the refreshment stands. If it weren't for them, there not only wouldn't be any winning Little League ball, there wouldn't be a Little League.

The ideal situation is to have experienced coaches, managers and umpires, if possible, but there is another indispensable quality that most of the men active in Little

League ball have in abundance—the know-how to handle boys not yet in their teens.

For many boys, this is going to be their first experience with discipline outside of the home. There is a minimum of discipline in their social lives, of course, except what their playmates enforce, and today's schools don't enforce the kind of discipline I knew as a boy. But on the Little League field he must do what his manager and coaches tell him—or face the consequences.

This, in its turn, imposes a burden on the men who run the team, one that most of them handle pretty well.

The manager and his coaches can't turn into a set of tyrants, setting up an arbitrary list of rules and demanding that every one of them be followed. There has to be a mixture of firmness and common sense, and every situation that arises has to be handled from that point of view.

You can't criticize a boy for being thrown out at first, obviously. But you should come down on him like a ton of bricks if he was thrown out because he figured the ball would be caught and he just dawdled his way down there, only to find that the fielder bobbled the ball and he would have been safe if he'd hustled.

I don't think you should ever criticize one player in front of others. Even in the case of the player who dawdled, the other players will be all over him without the coach saying a word. The coach should simply get that player after the game and tell him that one more performance like that and he will be out of the regular line-up.

Most Little League coaches know from the start that allowing a player to dawdle—even a valuable player—not only has its bad effects on the boy himself but it can affect the whole team. If it's allowed to go on long enough, it can turn a winning Little League team into a losing one.

One thing a manager should do in any decision affecting a player is to explain it to him. If it concerns more than one player—to them, in private.

It's inevitable that there will be jealousies and rivalries among the players on a Little League team, but the manager who is aware of this can do a good deal to keep them from getting out of hand by taking the trouble to explain the reasons he has for making the moves he does.

The time that words are needed most, in my opinion, is in making the toughest decision a Little League manager has to face: When to take out a pitcher who's gotten himself into really bad trouble.

Some managers think that it ruins a young pitcher's confidence to take him out after he's given up four successive base hits. This indicates that the manager doesn't believe the pitcher can recover from a bad spell. Other managers believe the opposite—that a young pitcher should be taken out when he's getting a real pasting.

I can't second guess a manager on a decision like that because I believe it depends so much on the boy himself. After all, situations like this arise in the majors, where the only criterion is winning the game, where the sensibilities of the pitcher don't enter into the manager's decision one way or the other. And the decisions are made one way or the other, depending on the circumstances of the game and that particular manager's way of thinking.

The only thing I have to say on the Little League decision is that the way the manager handles the pitcher is more important than what he does. If he just goes out and says: "Give me the ball," he's making a bad situation worse. If he says: "Johnny, you're having a tough spell that all pitchers go through and I have to stop this team, but you're still one of our top starting pitchers," he hasn't really made Johnny feel good—Johnny knows he's being shelled—but at least the manager has done the best he can not to undermine the boy's confidence.

In a funny way, kids are both tougher and more sensitive than adults think they are.

The only managers, and coaches, of whom I thoroughly

disapprove are the ones who act as though they were managing a major league team in a pennant race. They're always tense, always yelling their opinion of a play that one of their youngsters made on the field (generally bad), always ready to charge out of the dugout to yell at an umpire at the top of their voices on a close call.

Managers like these not only have a bad influence on the boys on their own team, they have a bad influence on all the youngsters on the field. In addition to that, they undermine the respect youngsters have for adults. What is any young boy going to think of a grown man charging out to the field, screaming at an umpire that a boy was safe when, in all probability, he was out; and the boys know it as well as the umpire?

I don't know how far a coach or a manager should go, in Little League, in trying to mold the boys under him. Subconsciously his very conduct is molding their minds all the time they play for him.

Some managers advocate talking to the boy's parents, if his conduct is bad enough—like using language that shouldn't be part of Little League ball. If that doesn't work the manager can always tell the boy that if he keeps talking that way, he won't play in the next game. And the game after that, if need be.

In my opinion, that's about as far as a manager can go in actually trying to "mold" a boy—except by the way he conducts himself.

I mentioned that I did not think a manager should allow himself to become a despot, and that goes for the amount of practice demanded of the boys, too.

I think that one two-hour session of practice a week is enough, and it's not a matter of life-and-death to make it up if it's rained out. Little League baseball should not be allowed to become a drudgery. The boys should look forward to practice. Not as much as to a game, of course, because practice can't possibly be as exciting, but as a time when they'll be together for a couple of hours, and they can work out difficulties they may be having. During practice, boys should also be able to have the undivided attention of a coach for a time, since at practice the manager is generally as busy as he is at a game.

The danger of having too much practice, or too long sessions, is that the boy will begin to lose interest in the game, just as he will if he's subject to too much pressure over a long period of time. I know a number of Little League managers, indeed, who hold only four or five practices during the entire season.

Their reasoning—and I have no quarrel with it at all—is that the Little League season normally starts in April, when the boys are still going to school and they have homework as well as their family life. And it ends in early July, when vacations have already started.

If a manager does schedule practice, however, I think that it should be run as strictly—or almost as strictly—as practice on a high school or college practice schedule. It should start on time and it should end on time. The various things to be practiced should be planned out in advance to the minute. It's amazing how much time you can waste figuring out what to do next if it isn't planned.

Summary

If I were allowed only one thing to say to adults about their role in making a winning Little League baseball team, I think it would be: Remember that the youngsters are at the age when they look on adults as their model for conduct.

Whether you're the manager, coach, umpire or simply a mother or father in the stands, remember that the youngsters—including your own son—are watching you and listening to you. If you fly off into a rage a boy has only one of two reactions. Either he thinks that's the thing to do, or else he's mortified at his father or mother for making a spectacle of themselves in front of all his friends and all the other people within hearing distance.

It's difficult for youngsters to display good sportsmanship when parents violate the rules, openly. Here we don't need model youngsters, we need model adults.

9

●●●●●●●●●●●●●●●●

THE LITTLE LEAGUE

By now, it is obvious that I am one hundred percent for the Little League. I know that every now and then there are articles in magazines questioning the value of Little League, and even a number of the people I meet think we should abandon it. It's too competitive, they are fond of saying, it puts too much stress on winning.

The simple answer, of course, is that all of life is competitive, and the stress on "winning" in adult life is complete. There are a few more points about Little League that I'd like to make:

1. THE NEGATIVE VALUE
2. THE BOY'S DEVELOPMENT
3. HIS CONTRIBUTIONS
4. COURAGE
5. THE LEAGUE ITSELF
6. A FINAL WORD

The Negative Value

I think the negative value of the Little League is so great that it becomes almost positive. By the negative value, I mean that if a boy is actively involved in playing organized ball, he obviously can't be running around the streets or hanging around the corner store getting into all sorts of trouble which is so easy to do.

The trouble-making kids he runs into will sneer at him for being a "jock"—or a ball player—but most Little Leaguers I've met take this in their stride. In fact, after a short while they became proud of it, especially if their local newspaper carries little accounts of Little League games.

The boys recognize very early that the jibes that are directed at them most frequently come from kids who couldn't make a Little League team, largely because these youngsters don't have the self discipline that is demanded to play ball.

We must remember, too, that man is a physical animal and as the sociologists keep telling us, he's a social animal. Being a physical animal, he's going to get involved in physical things, and being a social animal, he's going to get involved with his peers—whether in gangs or on teams.

All athletics are the best way I know of for taking care of a very important part of our bodily needs, physical activities. Team athletics, especially, fulfill the need for physical competitiveness that we're all born with. Little League gives the boy the physical activity he needs; it allows him to work off his physical competitiveness in a constructive rather than a destructive way, and it puts him on a team rather than into a gang.

The Boys Development

As I have already said, Little League helps to develop a boy morally in accord with the conduct that his manager and coaches set for him; it should also develop a sense of teamwork and sportsmanship.

It should play a major role in developing his body. A boy is still in the formative years at ten through twelve, and it's not too early for him to learn that he has to discipline his body. Playing Little League ball, he'll soon learn that if he isn't in condition, he won't be able to play up to his capabilities. As I said, in Little League the problem of a boy abusing himself with liquor or cigarettes or drugs is at an absolute minimum, thank the Lord! Even a simple thing like knowing if he stays up late watching television, he won't be able to play up to his best the next day, is a lesson that will stand him in good stead when he grows older.

A great contribution that I think Little League makes physically is that it begins to teach a boy to take care of his own body.

A good many of the youngsters who first come out for Little League have really had no physical training at all. They trip over their own feet, and if you ask them to throw a ball to you, you're lucky if it's within three feet.

It's amazing how they develop over a period of three years. You see development in the ability to hit, run, and the surprising amount of power that develops in this short period of time. Youngsters who come into the Little League with a kind of an off-balance walk, holding their hands as if they didn't know what to do with them—three years later you can just look at them and see that they know how to handle themselves.

His Contributions

I've talked about teamwork, and I've talked about the necessity for a youngster to put out to the best of his capacity, but I haven't talked about a quality that I think is inborn in youngsters—in everyone. That's the urge to feel that you're *contributing* to something.

I remember a discussion that a newspaperman once had with Bill Bradley, a star of the New York Knickerbocker basketball team, right after one of the Knick games.

On that occasion, Bill hadn't had an outstanding night, he hadn't scored the points that people have come to kind of expect from Bradley, and the newspaperman asked him point blank if he thought he'd played up to his best in the game.

Bradley's answer was that he felt that he had played up to the full limit of his ability, that he was doing what he always did on the court, playing the best he could. Even if he hadn't scored a lot of points, he said, he felt that he had contributed to the success of the team. (The Knicks had won.)

I think this sort of feeling is a wonderful quality for life. It's surprising how much better you feel if you're making a contribution of your own time and ability to something— whether it's your community or town or the school system or the Little League.

Courage

An advantage in playing a sport even with as little body contact as there is in Little League ball is the building up of courage, which, for most youngsters, means not showing fear. The batter who gets knocked down and gets up to dig his rear foot in is showing courage. Here is a place where the major leaguers are a good example. Everyone who watches baseball has seen a batter get knocked down, or hit by a pitch, or sustain even tougher hurts, and carry on right afterwards.

There's another type of courage that you don't see on the field but that the boy who plays ball knows all about. It's in the books that have been written about players like Mickey Mantle and others who have played day after day in actual physical pain.

I believe that you can learn courage, certainly physical courage. First you have to have confidence in yourself, in you ability to handle your own body. Then you build courage day by day, the same way that you develop your ability to concentrate, or your ability to make plays that a short while ago you wouldn't have dreamed of being able to make.

With courage, you take your first bumps and learn to

live with them, then you can handle tougher and tougher punishment. Finally, like, say, a football player or a hockey player you get to the point where one bump more or less doesn't make any difference.

Mickey Mantle is an outstanding example of a player with courage. Almost everyone knows the Mickey Mantle story, of course, how his legs were so bad that, especially in the later days of his career, they had to be taped almost every time he took the field to play. He'd grit his teeth, too. He played because he felt he could contribute to his team's success, that the welfare of the team was more important than the pain he felt.

When the time came that he felt he couldn't contribute enough to the team, because his legs had become so much of a handicap and he was not able to play up to the standards he set for himself, he retired. And that took courage itself, in a different way.

I remember a player, a pitcher named Lew Brissie. Brissie had a very bad leg, one so bad that you noticed it when he was walking, but he also had an overweening desire to play major league ball. Day after day and year after year he would grit his teeth and go out there and pitch off that bad leg, and after a while his sheer courage—or guts, if you want—paid off and he made it to the majors, where he had a very creditable career. I'm sorry that so few people remember, now.

The League Itself

I believe that the Little League is entitled to unstinted praise for the work it is doing for the boys of America, just under three million of whom are expected to be in Little League ball this year. The Federal Government itself has recognized the value of Little League ball, since it is the only sports organization in the country that operates under the sponsorship of a Federal charter, passed by both

Houses of Congress and signed by former President Lyndon B. Johnson.

I would like to touch on two things.

First, I wish every adult could visit the home of Little League baseball at Williamsport, Pennsylvania, at the time of the Little League World Series, as I had the opportunity to do a while back.

This world series was really an eye-opener for me. I had never seen it in operation before. Boys from various parts of the world, meeting each other, competing against each other, winning, losing, eating, sleeping in the same barracks, speaking different languages, but all there for the same basic purpose, to help their teams win.

You may have noticed yourself when you're watching a big league ball game how you tend to forget what color a ball player is, you're only interested in what he does. It was the same way with me at Williamsport.

Watching the game, I began to forget that this team came from Mexico or Japan or someplace in the United States. I became interested only in the kind of ball they were playing —which, for their age, was superb.

The year I was there, watching the youngsters who had won consoling the ones who had lost, the youngsters on both sides congratulating the boy who had just pitched a no-hitter, made me feel how great all these kids were. And if they could just carry all these values on into the adult world, how much better a place it would be in the future.

You see all these youngsters coming from different countries with different cultures, different languages and different religions, and you see that they have one thing in common— a love of baseball. You hope that this understanding they found in baseball will stay with them, when they go back to their homes, wherever they are. And that they all have something in common with other boys, no matter how great the differences may be.

I know that Little League ball isn't going to change the course of nations, but I believe that in today's strife-torn world, *anything* that contributes to understanding should be encouraged.

Little League boys are going to grow up to become the men who will help shape the future of their countries, and if the Little League lesson can be firmly implanted in their minds when they're ten, eleven, and twelve years old, I believe that it will stay with them when they're grown.

I would like to quote from the Little League handbook:

"It strives to inspire them (boys) with a goal and to enrich their lives towards the day when they must take their places in the world. It establishes for them rudiments of teamwork and fair play."

The second point that I wanted to make about the Little League concerns the boys who don't become one of the star players, or even one of the regular players, the ones the coach puts in only because he's dedicated to the proposal that every boy on the squad get a chance to be out on the field. I think that even these boys can get a great deal out of Little League ball.

A few years ago I ran into an extreme case of how youngsters who are physically below par can benefit. There's a wealthy gentleman in Indiana who got interested in the Little League and thought that its benefits should be carried further than to the average boy. He wanted to provide a league for boys who physically didn't have a prayer of making a regular Little League team. So he developed his own Little League, so to speak.

He provided the land for a playing field and had the field built, he provided the uniforms and the equipment, he got friends and neighbors to become managers and coaches and umpires, and he got major league ball players—and ex-ball players—to come out and talk to the youngsters. I was one of the latter and I saw these boys, all with physical handicaps of one sort or another. Some had bad legs, some had crippled arms, some were way underdeveloped.

But they all were motivated by a desire to play, and their spirit compared favorably with the spirit of any regular Little League team I've ever seen. That was the important thing, that and the sense that they were participating in something that was important to them.

I noticed that each one of these youngsters got a chance to play and that, only a relatively short space of time after the first teams had been created, there were enough youngsters applying so that a whole league was established. This is the sort of spirit, both on the part of the sponsor and of the boys themselves, that somehow to me epitomizes the spirit of Little League.

A Final Word

Life isn't a spectator sport.

One of the truly great things about the Little League is that it takes boys at their most impressionable age, and gets them out of the grandstands and down onto the playing fields.

If you're going to spend your whole life in the grandstand, just watching what goes on, its my opinion you're wasting your life.

If the Little League teaches youngsters nothing more than to stop watching and get to where the action is, it has justified its entire existence. It's the hope of the future.